FLORENCES' OVENWARE

from the
1920s
to the
PRESENT

Identification & Value Guide

Gene & Cathy Florence

COLLECTOR BOOKS
A Division of Schroeder Publishing Co., Inc.

Front Cover ~ McKee "Wild Rose" — Butter Dish, $60.00; Small Baker, $28.00; Large Baker, $35.00; Pyrex — 2 qt. Casserole, $14.00; Glassbake — 4" x 5" Oven/Fridge, $12.00 each; Cake Pan, angel food, $15.00; Federal — White Pitcher, 7½", 32 oz., $50.00; Mixing Bowl, 7", orange dots, $15.00; Mixing Bowl, 8⅛", green dots, $18.00; Pyrex — Santa Mug, $38.00.

Back Cover ~ McKee Mixing Bowls, 9", $25.00; 8", $20.00; 7", $15.00; 6", $10.00. Pyrex Carafe with Stand, $20.00; Pyrex Mug, $18.00.

Cover design • Beth Summers

Book design • Erica Weise

COLLECTOR BOOKS

P.O. Box 3009
Paducah, Kentucky 42002-3009
www.collectorbooks.com

The current values in this book should be used only as a guide. They are not intended to set prices, which vary from one section of the country to another. Auction prices as well as dealer prices vary greatly and are affected by condition as well as demand. Neither the authors nor the publisher assumes responsibility for any losses that might be incurred as a result of consulting this guide.

CONTENTS

ACKNOWLEDGMENTS

Ovenware pictured in this book came from many sources and several years of accumulating enough items to fill a book. There is no adequate way to thank Ron and Barbara Marks for their contributions. Ron has been searching in a three-state area for several years to help glean examples of Glasbake, Pyrex, and Federal items. I doubt I could come close to listing all of them pictured within. He had rummaged around for glass for the first Hazel-Atlas book as well. He enjoys the hunt, or so he keeps saying! We're certainly indebted to him for his finds!

Dan and Geri Tucker provided both glassware and photographs. They went out of their way to aid our quest as best as they could.

Kenn and Margaret Whitmyer were also kind enough to provide photographs. Thanks to them and thanks to Mary O'Donnell, also.

Thanks to all the other dealers and collectors who provided us with catalogs and tidbits of information when they found out we were working on this book.

Photography was accomplished in a two year interval by Charley Lynch and Richard Walker. Several sessions lasted for seemingly unending days at a time. I heard more than once, "You mean there's more?" as we unloaded more boxes at the studio.

INTRODUCTION

We had been asked to write a book on Pyrex by collectors and dealers for years. Since there were books available on that subject, we resisted. Finally, we saw a need to explore the companies who competed with Pyrex, and so this ovenware book concept was born. We've lost count of the requests to add information about Federal glass. Hopefully, we have provided a beginning toward that end. This book is divided into sections by company. Each company is subdivided by patterns and then by items within that company. Luckily, most company designations are embossed or labeled on items, so even beginning collectors can identify company of origin. Everyone has heard of Pyrex and Fire-King, but there were other companies competing for consumer funds. Notably, Federal used the idea of Heat Proof ovenware, which carried over into its dinnerware patterns, to challenge Fire-King's ovenware. Fire-King was also matching oven dishes to its dinnerware lines.

Most of Hocking's dinnerware patterns were advertised as heat resistant, heat proof, or ovenproof. Hocking provided baking dishes, casseroles, refrigerator storage containers, and cups, saucers, and dinner plates with the same designs. A housewife could choose one pattern and have all bakeware match the dishes she served on. Many patterns were advertised as usable from the refrigerator to the oven and then to the table. Do not try this with a microwave oven, since pre-1990 ovenware items were not made to withstand drastic temperature changes. For that matter, a majority of the ovenware had labels or imprinting in the glass cautioning it was not suitable for stove top or broiler use. Most Fire-King mugs can be used in microwaves, but beware of extreme temperature changes. You can test for microwave compatibility by putting a dish in one for 10 seconds and seeing if the dish gets hot. If it does, it may not withstand microwaving.

Federal's ovenware was not as widely distributed as its competitors, so it is not as plentiful. You will find mixing bowl sets with matching mugs. Tumblers were made in some patterns, but these are not heat proof! Federal mugs are more collected than any other Federal items. Souvenir and advertising mugs are at the forefront with collectors. Most Federal mugs are marked with an *F* in a shield and "Heat Proof." We have provided some catalog pages so you can see the handle shapes of Federal mugs. Those handle shapes will help in identifying unmarked mugs.

Glasbak was the original spelling for McKee's ovenware, but was changed to *Glasbake* sometime later. Jeannette took over the old McKee factory when Thatcher Glass sold it in the early 1960s. Many Glasbake mugs are marked "Heat Resistant" rather than "Oven Proof." Different terminologies were used over the years. Most heavier mugs can withstand use in the microwave, but always test (explained previously). Glasbake patterns had pieces that served in oven or refrigerator. Too, a few refrigerator-only items are pictured, but there are ovenware items that are found in that same pattern. When buying items to illustrate designs, you have to purchase what is found! Unfortunately, we sometimes saw a high-priced item that we passed on and never saw again! A few damaged pieces are shown for illustration.

Pyrex is a familiar name that most people recognize whether they are collectors or not. As with Fire-King, almost every home had a piece or two. Sometimes it was handed down by a relative. My mom used the large yellow 4-quart bowl from the 4-bowl colored mixing set almost as often as she did the Fire-King Sapphire blue roaster half. Pyrex has worldwide distribution today. You can find pieces in this country that are marked "France" or "England." Some examples are pictured at the end of the Pyrex section.

PRICING

Ovenware pricing is determined by condition and rarity. Condition is more important, because this glass was made to be used — and it was. Finding older, unused pieces adds a premium to the price, as does finding pieces with original labels or boxes. Prices within this book are for items "gently" used, with full color and no chips or cracks. A few light scratches inside are tolerable, but no heavy wear is allowed. Items with faded or missing colors or extreme usage marks will fetch 25 – 40% of the prices listed — if wanted at all. Even rare items will seldom bring more than 50% if worn. Collectors are looking for quality. People buying for use or sentimentality may buy lesser quality, but are not going to pay premium prices.

MEASUREMENTS

Measurements in this book are from catalog listings or our actual measurements. Some items are embossed on the bottom as to size or capacity. All measurements are without handles unless otherwise noted. Some Pyrex catalogs emphasize that all measurements are without handles, so we did the same for all companies.

Federal Glass Company, 1900 – 1984

This section includes Federal's Heat Proof dinnerware lines that were in direct competition to Anchor-Hocking's Fire-King patterns. The Federal *F* in a shield symbol is on nearly every piece photographed in this section. Almost all Federal Heat Proof is white in color, which is the basic background against which fired-on colors were applied. Be aware that many of the applied patterns on white wore off with use. There are several cross-over (like) patterns among Federal and Fire-King wares, as well as among those of Federal and Glasbake.

Fewer crystal pieces were produced by Federal than by other ovenware manufacturing companies. Federal made large amounts of advertising mugs, as well as a limited edition run of mugs (250) to commemorate Martin Luther King. This mug may well be the most desired of any Federal mug. A notation for beginners is that any item listed as "from the morgue" refers to an item from a storage area at Federal (et al.) where experimental or sample items were stored.

Patterns – *Blossom*

Bowls	
#248, 9", crystal, mixing	$10.00
#814, 9", rust, mixing/baking	$18.00
#812, 8", brown, mixing/baking	$15.00
#815, 7⅛", yellow, mixing/baking	$12.00
#813, 6", avocado, mixing/baking	$10.00
#245, 5", crystal, mixing	$2.50

From *It's All in the Federal Glass* 1977 catalog, p. 84.

From *Federal Glass '79: The Great Looks of Success,* p. 100.

Patterns – *Bouquet*, Decoration #1410

Bouquet
White Ware

	L	M	N	O	P	Q	R	S	T
	W236/1410	**W237/1410**	**W238/1410**	**W278/1410**	**W279/1410**	**W280/1410**	**W281/1410**	**W2723/1410**	**W2745/1410**
	6"	7"	8"	1¼ qt.	1½ qt.	8"	6 oz.	1½ qt.	2½ qt.
	Mix-Bake Bowl	Mix-Bake Bowl	Mix-Bake Bowl	Loaf Pan	Utility Dish	Round Cake	Custard	Covered Casserole	Covered Casserole
Bulk Packs	1 Dz. 12 lbs.	1 Dz. 20 lbs.	1 Dz. 23 lbs.	½ Dz. 11 lbs.	½ Dz. 14 lbs.	½ Dz. 10 lbs.	4 Dz. 16 lbs.	6 Sets 16 lbs.	6 Sets 24 lbs.

From *Federal Glass '76* catalog, p. 77.

Loaf pan, 278/1410, 1¼ qt., $12.00
Custard, W281/1410, 6 oz., $4.00

From *Federal Glassware Catalog No. 60,* p. 33.

Federal Glass Company advertisement for Clover Blossom.

Burgundy and Clover Blossom

	Item	Price
1	Plate, 11¼", coupe chop	$12.00
2	Plate, 10", coupe	$8.00
3	Bowl, 8", rim soup	$10.00
4	Cup	$3.00
5	Saucer	$.50
6	Bowl, 4⅞", dessert	$3.50
7	Sugar, with cover	$10.00
8	Creamer	$5.00

Patterns – *Country Kitchen (Tablecloth)*, Decoration #2025

Back row:
1 Casserole, 2½ qt. (cover missing) $15.00
2 Bowl, 9", mixing/baking $15.00
3 Custard, 6 oz. $4.00
4 Bowl, 8", mixing/baking $12.00

Front row:
5 Bowl, 5", cereal $7.00
6 Utility dish, 1½ qt. $12.00
7 Mug, 9½ oz. $8.00

Bakeware

Federal's recipe for today's cook-at-home enthusiasts.
Start with extra durable Durawhite items, decorate with one of two colorful stylings. Mix them in a variety of functional shapes and sizes.
Serve individually or in eye-catching packaging.

Tablecloth
White Ware

	A	B	C	D	E	F	G	H	I	J	K
	W222/2025	**W227/2025**	**W237/2025**	**W238/2025**	**W239/2025**	**W278/2025**	**W279/2025**	**W280/2025**	**W281/2025**	**W2723/2025**	**W2745/2025**
	5" Cereal	9½ oz. Mug	7" Mix-Bake Bowl	8" Mix-Bake Bowl	9" Mix-Bake Bowl	1¼ qt. Loaf Pan	1½ qt. Utility Dish	8" Round Cake Dish	6 oz. Custard	1½ qt. Covered Casserole	2½ qt. Covered Casserole
Bulk Packs	2 Dz. 13 lbs.	2 Dz. 14 lbs.	1 Dz. 20 lbs.	1 Dz. 23 lbs.	1 Dz. 30 lbs.	½ Dz. 11 lbs.	½ Dz. 14 lbs.	½ Dz. 10 lbs.	4 Dz. 16 lbs.	6 Sets 16 lbs.	6 Sets 24 lbs.

White Ware Has Extra Durability

Federal Durawhite items are made of heat-resistant borosilicate glass. This helps prevent expansion and cracking of the glass during temperature changes.

(B-43)
13-Pc. Country Kitchen Bake-Serve Set
One each: 1½ qt. Utility, 2½ qt. Covered Casserole, 1¼ qt. Loaf, 8" Round Cake, eight 6 oz. Custards. Packed in colorful individual carton.
1 Set, 13 lbs.

From *Federal Glass '76* catalog, p. 76.

Patterns – *Fruit Fare,* Decoration #6445

Federal Glass Company advertisement for Fruit Fare.

Mixing bowl, #236, 6", $10.00

Patterns – *"Fruit & Floral"*

Bowl, 8", mixing	$12.00
Bowl, 9", mixing	$15.00
Loaf pan, 10" x 5"	$15.00

Patterns – *Golden Berry*

Plate, W253, 9"	$3.00
Bowl, W254, 4⅞", dessert	$3.00
Bowl, W255, 8½"	$7.00
Bowl, 7", soup	$5.00

Patterns – *Golden Glory,* *Decoration #100, c. 1961*

No.	Item	Price
9	Bowl, W254, 4⅞", dessert	$4.50
12	Bowl, W257, 8", rimmed soup	$12.00
4	Bowl, W255, 8½", vegetable	12.00
8	Creamer, W258	$5.00
10	Cup, W250	$3.50
1	Plate, W252, 7¾", salad	$3.00
2	Plate, W253, 9⅛", dinner	$5.00
7	Platter, W260, 12", oval	$12.00
11	Saucer, W251	$.50
5	Sugar, W259	$4.00
6	Sugar lid	$4.00
3	Tumbler, 10 oz., 5"	$10.00

This decoration is also found on Federal's Dutch Garden blank issued in 1978. The triangular labels proclaim "Heat-Proof." We have supplied catalog numbers where known.

Greenbrier

Dinnerware lines that combine functional design with colorful accents all at economy-minded price points. As bulk items or in a variety of sets, these lines offer attractive merchandising and promotional opportunities.

Greenbrier

	A	B	C	D	E	F	G	H	I	J
	W450/116	**W451/116**	**W454/116**	**W457/116**	**W455/116**	**W258/116**	**W459/116**	**W461/116**	**W462/116**	**W463/116**
			4⅞"	6⅜"	8½"			11¼"	7⅞"	10"
	Greenbrier Cup	Greenbrier Saucer	Greenbrier Dessert	Greenbrier Soup/Cereal	Greenbrier Vegetable Bowl	Greenbrier Creamer	Greenbrier Covered Sugar	Greenbrier Chop plate	Greenbrier Salad Plate	Greenbrier Dinner Plate
Bulk Packs	3 Dz. 14 lbs.	3 Dz. 16 lbs.	3 Dz. 13 lbs.	3 Dz. 25 lbs.	1 Dz. 16 lbs.	1 Dz. 6 lbs.	1 Dz. 9 lbs.	1 Dz. 23 lbs.	3 Dz. 27 lbs.	2 Dz. 32 lbs.

From *Federal Glass '76* catalog, p. 70.

C Bowl, 4⅞", dessert	$4.00
D Bowl, 6⅜", soup/cereal	$8.00
E Bowl, 8½", vegetable	$12.00
F Creamer	$5.00
A Cup	$4.00
I Plate, 7⅞", salad	$4.00
J Plate, 10" dinner	$8.00
H Plate, 11¼" chop	$12.00
B Saucer	$1.00
G Sugar, w/cover	$10.00

Patterns – *Moon Glow*, Decoration #113

Moonglow

Dinnerware lines that combine functional design with colorful accents all at economy-minded price points. As bulk items or in a variety of sets, these lines offer attractive merchandising and promotional opportunities.

K L M N O P Q R S T

Moon Glow

	K	L	M	N	O	P	Q	R	S	T
	W450/113	**W451/113**	**W454/113**	**W457/113**	**W455/113**	**W258/113**	**W459/113**	**W461/113**	**W462/113**	**W463/113**
			4⅞"	6⅜"	8½"			11¼"	7⅝"	10"
	Moon Glow Cup	Moon Glow Saucer	Moon Glow Dessert	Moon Glow Soup/Cereal	Moon Glow Vegetable Bowl	Moon Glow Creamer	Moon Glow Covered Sugar	Moon Glow Chop Plate	Moon Glow Salad Plate	Moon Glow Dinner Plate
Bulk Packs	3 Dz. 14 lbs.	3 Dz. 16 lbs.	3 Dz. 13 lbs.	3 Dz. 25 lbs.	1 Dz. 16 lbs.	1 Dz. 6 lbs.	1 Dz. 9 lbs.	1 Dz. 23 lbs.	3 Dz. 27 lbs.	2 Dz. 32 lbs.

From *Federal Glass '76* catalog, p. 71.

Commemorative plate, 7⅝", "Best Wishes, William Schneider, Chairman" (Republican Party?), $10.00

Items from Federal morgue, rare dinnerware.

No.	Item	Price
6	Creamer	$10.00
7	Cup	$5.00
1	Plate, 8¼"	$7.00
2	Plate, 11½"	$10.00
8	Saucer	$2.00
3	Sherbet	$8.00
5	Sugar	$10.00
4	Tumbler, 10 oz., 4¾"	$12.00

Patterns – *"Maple Leaves"*

Item	Price
Batter bowl	$35.00
Bowl, 7 1/16"	$10.00
Casserole, 1½ qt.	$12.00
Refrigerator dish, 8¾" (Fire-King)	$16.00

Patterns – *"Moss Brown"*

Item	Price
Top row:	
Casserole, 2½ qt., w/lid	$10.00
Plate, 11¼"	$6.00
Saucer	$1.00
Cup	$3.00
Plate, 10"	$4.00
Sugar with lid	$7.00
Bottom row:	
Bowl, 7½", soup	$5.00
Bowl, 8½", vegetable	$6.00
Bowl, 4⅞", dessert	$2.00
Loaf pan, 1¼ qt.	$7.00

Patterns – *"Star"*

Batter bowl, $45.00

Mixing bowl, 8", $13.00

Patterns – *White Camellia,* c. 1956

	Item	Price
7	Bowl, W214, 4⅞", dessert	$2.50
6	Bowl, W217, 8", rimmed soup	$6.00
1	Creamer, W218	$3.00
4	Cup, W210	$3.00
2	Plate, W212, 7¾", salad	$3.00
3	Plate, W213, 9⅛", dinner	$5.00
	Saucer, W211	$1.00
5	Sugar, W219, without cover	$3.00

White Camellia
starter set, in box, $55.00

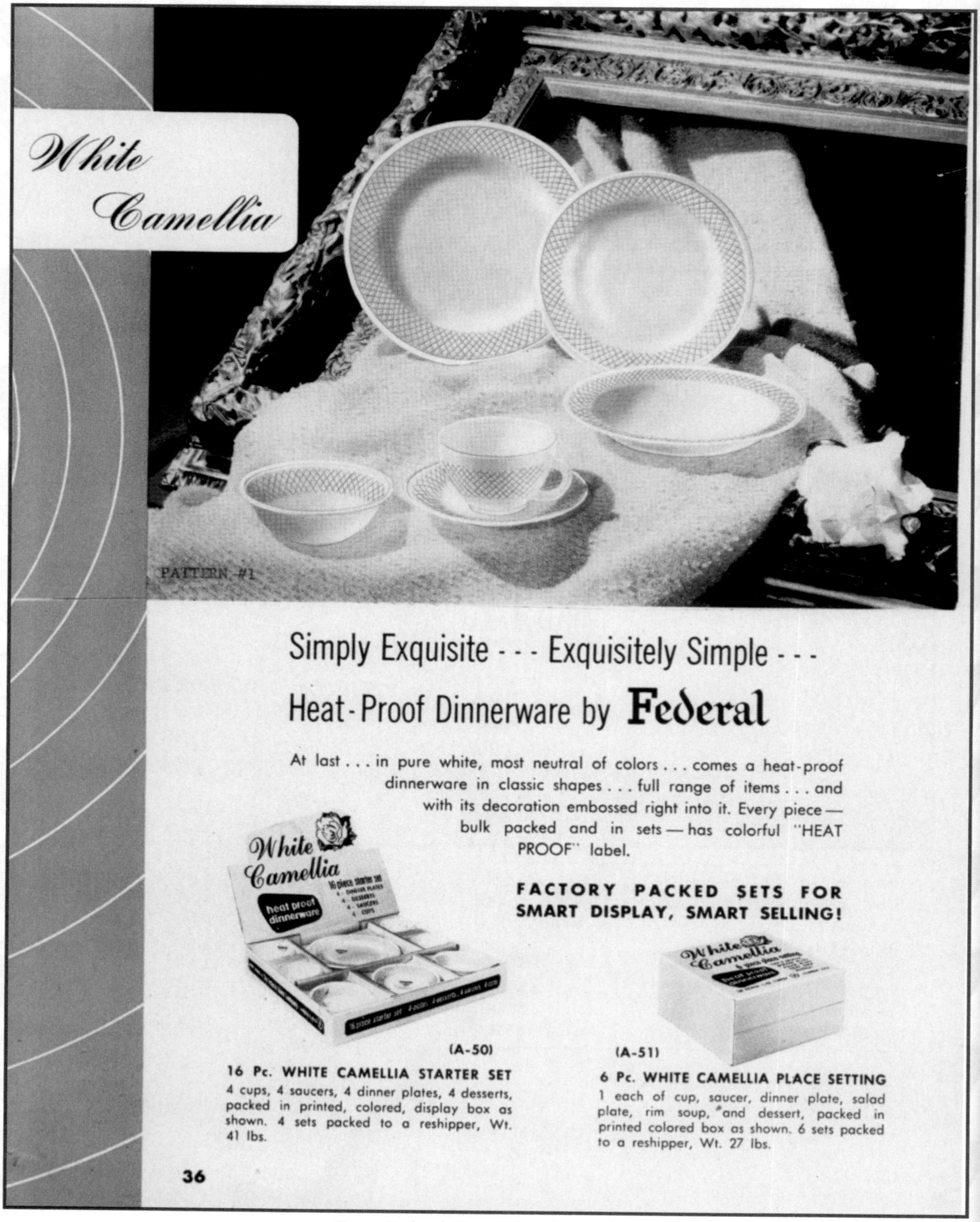

White Camellia

PATTERN #1

Simply Exquisite - - - Exquisitely Simple - - -
Heat-Proof Dinnerware by **Federal**

At last . . . in pure white, most neutral of colors . . . comes a heat-proof dinnerware in classic shapes . . . full range of items . . . and with its decoration embossed right into it. Every piece — bulk packed and in sets — has colorful "HEAT PROOF" label.

FACTORY PACKED SETS FOR SMART DISPLAY, SMART SELLING!

(A-50)

16 Pc. WHITE CAMELLIA STARTER SET
4 cups, 4 saucers, 4 dinner plates, 4 desserts, packed in printed, colored, display box as shown. 4 sets packed to a reshipper, Wt. 41 lbs.

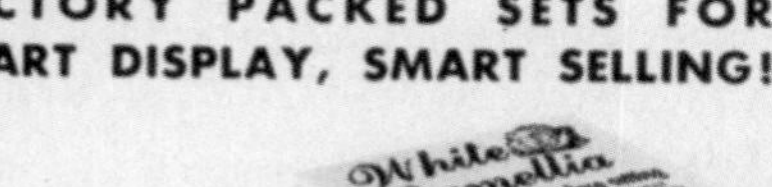

(A-51)

6 Pc. WHITE CAMELLIA PLACE SETTING
1 each of cup, saucer, dinner plate, salad plate, rim soup, and dessert, packed in printed colored box as shown. 6 sets packed to a reshipper, Wt. 27 lbs.

36

From *Federal Glass '56* catalog, p. 36.

WHITE CAMELLIA BULK PACKED

W210
CUP
Pkd. 6 doz. ctn. Wt. 30 lbs.

W211
SAUCER
Pkd. 6 doz. ctn. Wt. 29 lbs.

W212—7¾"
SALAD PLATE
Pkd. 3 doz. ctn. Wt. 26 lbs.

W213—9⅛"
DINNER PLATE
Pkd. 3 doz. ctn. Wt. 37 lbs.

W214—4⅞"
DESSERT
Pkd. 6 doz. ctn. Wt. 25 lbs.

W217—8"
RIM SOUP
Pkd. 3 doz. ctn. Wt. 29 lbs.

W215—8½"
BOWL OR VEGETABLE
Pkd. 1 doz. ctn. Wt. 15 lbs.

W218—
CREAMER
Pkd. 3 doz. ctn. Wt. 16 lbs.

W219—
COVERED SUGAR
Pkd. 3 doz. pr. ctn. Wt. 22 lbs.

W220—12"
OVAL PLATTER
Pkd. 1 doz. ctn. Wt. 21 lbs.

37

From *Federal Glass '56* catalog, p. 7.

#2723, 1½ qt., 6½" w x 4½" t, $10.00

#2745, 2½ qt., 8", $12.00
#2723, 1½ qt., 6⅝", $10.00

Sprayed color (see p. 32), 8", $12.00

W229, 5", $5.00

2½ qt., 8", $10.00
1 cup, 4⅛", $4.00

1½ qt., 6½" w x 4½" h, $10.00

"Compliments of Farmers Cooperative Co…Barnes City, Iowa," front view, 6⅞", $30.00

Reverse of bowl

"Dennis R. Boldt, Your Oak Grove Milkman…Mt. Lake, Minn.," #237, 7", $20.00

"McDonnell Feed Store…Bernard, Iowa," #237, 7", $20.00; #238, 8", $25.00

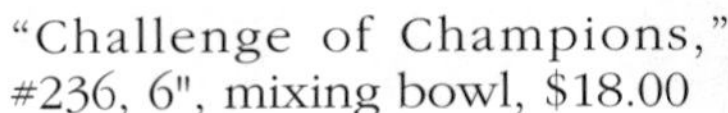

"Challenge of Champions," #236, 6", mixing bowl, $18.00

Items – *Bowls, Mixing*

#236, 6"	$10.00
#235, 5"	$6.00
#237, 7"	$12.00
#238, 8⅛"	$15.00
#239, 9 3/16"	$18.00

#237, 7" $10.00
#238, 8⅛" . . .$12.00
#239, 9 3/16" . . .$15.00

6", yellow dots $12.00
7", orange dots $15.00
8⅛", green dots $18.00
9 3/16", green dots $20.00

7" $15.00
9 1/16" $22.00
5", cereal $10.00
6" $12.00

Items – *Bowls & Mugs*

Mug, 9½" oz., $12.00
Bowl, 5", $10.00

Raggedy Ann & Andy bowl, 5 1/16", $15.00
Raggedy Ann & Andy mug, 3¼" h, $15.00
Set, $35.00

Items – *Miscellaneous*

Creamer, floral	$6.00
Sugar, floral	$6.00
Sugar, plain	$3.00
Sugar with lid, Avon	$15.00
Sugar, coffee klatch	$12.00

Pitcher, 7½" h, 32 oz., from morgue, $50.00

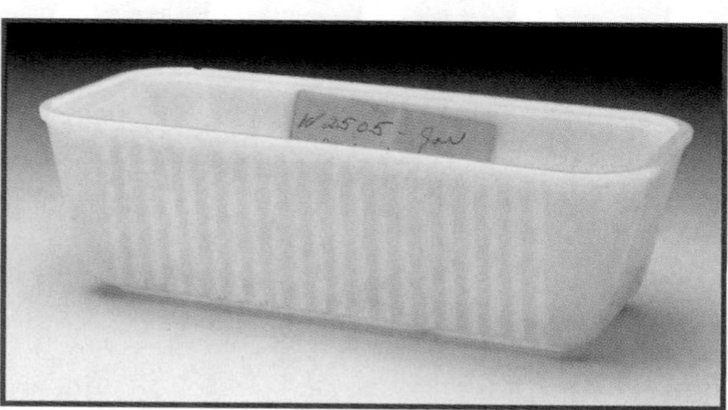

Loaf pan, W2505, 8" x 4", from morgue, $18.00

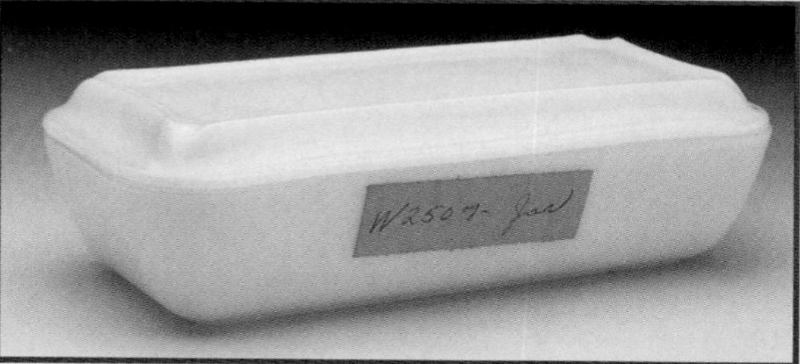

Jar, W2507, from morgue, with lid, $30.00

Christmas plate, 9⅞", $15.00

Top row:
W309, 11 oz.
Dutch (design also in mixing bowls set) . . . .$12.50 each
Calico, red and green $6.00 each

Bottom row:
W309, 11 oz.
Souvenir mugs . . . .$8.00 each
(higher prices for local collectors)
"Moss Brown" $4.00

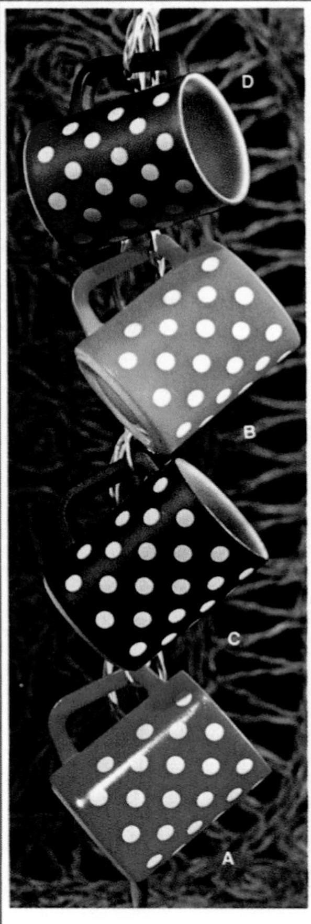

	Polka Dots				Calico				Warm Colors			
	A	B	C	D	E	F	G	H	I	J	K	L
	W309/2785	**W309/2787**	**W309/2788**	**W309/2789**	**W309/2435**	**W309/2436**	**W309/2437**	**W309/2438**	**W310/812**	**W310/813**	**W310/814**	**W310/815**
	11 oz.	11 oz.	11 oz.	11 oz.	11 oz.	11 oz.	11 oz.	11 oz.	10 oz.	10 oz.	10 oz.	10 oz.
									Country	Country	Country	Country
	Mug	Mug	Mug	Mug	Mug	Mug	Mug	Mug	Mug	Mug	Mug	Mug
	Dec.	Dec.	Dec.	Dec.	Dec.	Dec.	Dec.	Dec.	Dec.	Dec.	Dec.	Dec.
	Red	Orange	Black	Brown	Red	Blue	Green	Brown	Dark Brown	Avocado	Rust	Yellow
	Polka Dots	Polka Dots	Polka Dots	Polka Dots	Calico	Calico	Calico	Calico				
Bulk	2 Dz.	2 Dz.	2 Dz.	2 Dz.	2 Dz.	2 Dz.	2 Dz.	2 Dz.	1 Dz.	1 Dz.	1 Dz.	1 Dz.
Packs	18 lbs.	18 lbs.	18 lbs.	18 lbs.	18 lbs.	18 lbs.	18 lbs.	18 lbs.	11 lbs.	11 lbs.	11 lbs.	11 lbs.
									•	•	•	•

Mugs

A vast variety that puts a handle on selling opportunities—geared to current consumer buying trends with nature and nostalgia decs and colors.

• **NEW**

W227 Mugs

	Tablecloth	Blue Willow
	X	Y
	W227/2025	**W227/2730**
	9½ oz.	9½ oz.
	Stacking Mug	Stacking Mug
	Dec. Tablecloth	Dec. Blue Willow
Bulk	2 Dz.	2 Dz.
Packs	14 lbs.	14 lbs.

W309 Mugs

	Zodiac
	Z
	W309(A)/1250
	11 oz.
	Stacking Mug
	Assorted two ea. of the 12 signs of the Zodiac
Bulk	2 Dz.
Packs	18 lbs.

From *Federal Glass '76* catalog, p. 72.

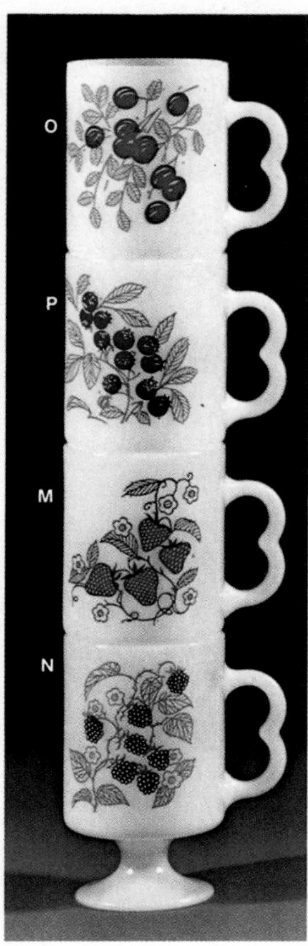

	Berries				Flowers			Garden Scenes			
	M	N	O	P	Q	R	S	T	U	V	W
	W314/2445	**W314/2450**	**W314/2451**	**W314/2452**	**W227/3080**	**W227/3085**	**W227/3090**	**W309/2440**	**W309/2441**	**W309/2442**	**W309/2443**
	9 oz.	9 oz.	9 oz.	9 oz.	9½ oz.	9½ oz.	9½ oz.	11 oz.	11 oz.	11 oz.	11 oz.
	Mug	Mug	Mug	Mug	Stacking Mug	Stacking Mug	Stacking Mug	Mug	Mug	Mug	Mug
	Dec. Strawberries	Dec. Raspberries	Dec. Cranberries	Dec. Blueberries	Dec. Daffodils	Dec. Poppies	Dec. Roses	Dec. Strawberry Patch	Dec. Melon Patch	Dec. Watermelon Patch	Dec. Banana Tree
Bulk Packs	2 Dz. 16 lbs.	2 Dz. 16 lbs.	2 Dz. 16 lbs.	2 Dz. 16 lbs.	1 Dz. 7 lbs. ●	1 Dz. 7 lbs. ●	1 Dz. 7 lbs. ●	2 Dz. 18 lbs.	2 Dz. 18 lbs.	2 Dz. 18 lbs.	2 Dz. 18 lbs.

FW308/9210
Four 8 oz. Continental Cups in die-cut carton that displays the ware and contains exciting hot drink recipes on center divider. Finger holes add carry-home ease. Order by item number shown in Four Pak section of chart. Include item description for absolute identification.

AA
W227(A)/3065
9½ oz.
Stacking Mug
Assorted one ea. of the 12 signs of the Zodiac
Bulk Packs 1 Dz. 7 lbs.
●

BB
W299/405
11 oz.
Beer Stein
Dec. Indescent
Bulk Packs 2 Dz. 26 lbs.

CC
W308/9210
8 oz.
Continental Cup
Dec. Irish Coffee
Bulk Packs 2 Dz. 16 lbs.
FW308/9210
Four Packs 6 Sets 15 lbs.

● **NEW**

From *Federal Glass '76* catalog, p. 73.

W229 Bowls
Sprayed Colors

	A	B	C	D
	W229/812	**W229/813**	**W229/475**	**W229/478**
	5" Bowl Dec. Dark Brown	5" Bowl Dec. Avocado	5" Bowl Dec. Red	5" Bowl Dec. Yellow
Bulk Packs	1 Dz. 8 lbs.	1 Dz. 8 lbs.	1 Dz. 8 lbs.	1 Dz. 8 lbs.
	•	•		

W228 Mugs
Sprayed Colors

	E	F	G	H
	W228/812	**W228/813**	**W228/475**	**W228/478**
	9½ oz. Stacking Mug Dec. Dark Brown	9½ oz. Stacking Mug Dec. Avocado	9½ oz. Stacking Mug Dec. Red	9½ oz. Stacking Mug Dec. Yellow
Bulk Packs	1 Dz. 7 lbs.	1 Dz. 7 lbs.	1 Dz. 7 lbs.	1 Dz. 7 lbs.
	•	•		

W222 Bowls
Sprayed Colors

	I	J	K	L
	W222/812	**W222/813**	**W222/814**	**W222/815**
	5" Bowl Dec. Dark Brown	5" Bowl Dec. Avocado	5" Bowl Dec. Rust	5" Bowl Dec. Yellow
Bulk Packs	2 Dz. 13 lbs.	2 Dz. 13 lbs.	2 Dz. 13 lbs.	2 Dz. 13 lbs.
	•	•	•	•

W227 Mugs
Sprayed Colors

	M	N	O	P
	W227/812	**W227/813**	**W227/814**	**W227/815**
	9½ oz. Stacking Mug Dec. Dark Brown	9½ oz. Stacking Mug Dec. Avocado	9½ oz. Stacking Mug Dec. Rust	9½ oz. Stacking Mug Dec. Yellow
Bulk Packs	2 Dz. 14 lbs.	2 Dz. 14 lbs.	2 Dz. 14 lbs.	2 Dz. 14 lbs.
	•	•	•	•

W310
Country Mug
Meets the demand for "basics"—utilitarian items that sell year 'round—with design that appeals to consumer preferences for the look and feel of yesterday.

• **NEW**

Oven-Proof Glassware
Dura-White

	Q	R	S	T	U	V	W	X	Y	Z	AA
	W228	**W227**	**W200**	**W314**	**W299**	**W309**	**W310**	**W308**	**W216**	**W222**	**W229**
	9½ oz. Stacking Mug	9½ oz. Stacking Mug	8 oz. Mug	9 oz. Footed Mug	11 oz. Beer Stein	11 oz. Continental Stacking Mug	10 oz. Country Mug	8 oz. Continental Cup	5" Bowl	5" Bowl	5" Bowl
Bulk Packs	1 Dz. 7 lbs.	2 Dz. 14 lbs.	2 Dz. 15 lbs.	2 Dz. 16 lbs.	2 Dz. 26 lbs.	2 Dz. 18 lbs.	1 Dz. 11 lbs.	2 Dz. 16 lbs.	2 Dz. 16 lbs.	2 Dz. 13 lbs.	1 Dz. 8 lbs.
							•				

From *Federal Glass '76* catalog, p. 74.

From *Federal Glass '74* catalog, p. 76.

Dogpatch, $25.00
Zodiac, $10.00

Santa, $25.00

Astronaut, W922, front view, $25.00

Astronaut, W922, back view

Indiana Centennial, $7.00

Indiana Centennial, back view

Top row:		**Bottom row:**	
W314, 9oz.		W314, 9oz.	
Sea World	$10.00	"I Lost My A...in Reno"	$10.00
Donald Duck	$15.00	Berry Decorations	$8.00
Pluto	$15.00	Our Lady of Angels High School 50th Anniversary	$10.00
Minnie Mouse	$18.00	Pandora Gilboa Bicentennial, Ohio	$10.00
King's Island	$10.00	Red Pig Inn, Ottawa, Ohio	$10.00

Items – *Mugs*

Continential cups, all W308, 8 oz., $8.00 each

Continential cups, W308, 8 oz., $8.00 each

NASA Space Shuttle, 5½", marked "RCA," $20.00
Red and blue, 5½" h, $4.00 each

Top row:
W227, 9½ oz.
- Six Flags $8.00
- Opryland $8.00
- New York City, Twin Towers $15.00
- Kennywood Park, Pittsburgh, Pa. $6.00
- Great Smoky Mountains .. $6.00

Center row:
W227, 9½ oz.
- New York World's Fair .$15.00
- British Columbia $6.00
- Sprayed color $6.00
- Plymouth, Mass. $6.00
- Plains, Georgia, Carter .$35.00

Bottom row:
W227, 9½ oz.
- Beatles, front back view $60.00
- Chintz blue (orange, red, brown) $6.00
- Christmas 1978 .... $15.00
- Daffodils $12.00

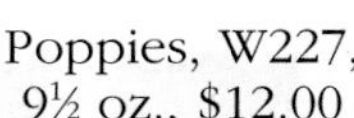

Poppies, W227, 9½ oz., $12.00

Christmas, W227, 9½ oz., 1975 – 1978, $15.00 each

Top row:
W227, 9½ oz.
"I Had a Bad Idea," front view $6.00
"Reynolds Metals Bad Guy," back view $6.00
"Truck and Trailer Supply… Cincinnati, Ohio" $6.00
"Truck and Trailer Supply…Cincinnati, Ohio," second style $6.00
1885 Moor Man's $6.00

Center row:
W227, 9½ oz.
"Arby's" $12.00
"FSU, Red Lobster" $12.00
"Enjoy Health, Eat Your Honey" (Risque?) $15.00
"PBA" $6.00
"An Evening with Gerald Ford and Donald Lukens, July 12, 1968" $15.00

Bottom row:
W227, 9½ oz.
"World's Greatest Grandma" $6.00
Heat Proof $6.00
Blue Willow $12.00
"M" $6.00
Comic $10.00

Mickey Mouse,
W227, 9½ oz., $25.00

Minnie Mouse,
back view of Mickey

Top row:
- Paneled Blue, 8 oz. $5.00
- Paneled White, 8 oz. $10.00
- W310, Country sprayed
  - Avacado, #813 . . . .$5.00
  - Rust, #814 . . . .$5.00
  - Yellow, #815 . . . .$5.00

Center row:
- W200, 8 oz.
  - "Autocar Runabout, 1902" $15.00
  - "Selden's Motor Wagon, 1877' $15.00
  - "Winton Automobile, 1898" $15.00
  - "Duryea's Motor Wagon, 1895" $15.00
  - "Bonanza Sirloin Pit" $8.00

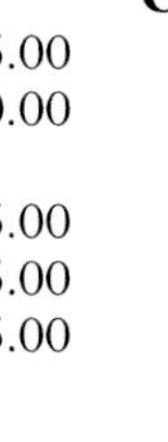

Bottom row:
- W228, 9½ oz.
  - Green $4.00
  - Red $4.00
  - Blue $4.00
  - Red, white, and blue $10.00
  - Liberty Bell $10.00

Paneled mug, $5.00

Dr. Martin Luther King, W227, rare, only 250 made, $150.00

Sportsman Series	
Tumbler, Ring Neck Pheasant	$8.00
Tumbler, 5⅞", Mallard	$8.00
Mug, W227, 9½ oz., Canada Goose (Grouse)	$10.00
Mug, W227, 9½ oz., Ring Neck Pheasant (Mallard)	$10.00

Yellow, W228, $6.00

Yellow, back view

FIRE-KING
by Anchor-Hocking, 1941 – 2000

Anchor-Hocking ovenware lines were issued under the Fire-King label. Many pieces were thus imprinted in the glassware itself, but some only carried paper labels. We have included many of the popular dinnerware lines (marked "Oven Ware") that are collected, but there are additional patterns that can be found. Some others are pictured in our *Anchor-Hocking's Fire-King and More* book.

As with Federal wares, Hocking's decaled designs on white have a tendency to flake or fade from dishwasher and cleanser use. The first Anchor-Hocking ovenware line of Heat Proof Sapphire blue was introduced in 1941, and later ovenware was made appropriate for both oven and microwave. Microwavable items are marked. Do not use ovenware items in the microwave unless so marked.

Patterns – "*Bubble*," 1941 – 1968

"Beautifully designed tableware that can be used in the oven, on the table, in the refrigerator."

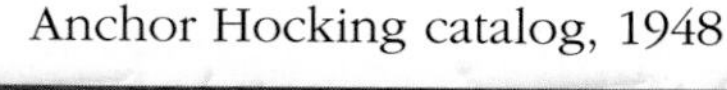
Anchor Hocking catalog, 1948

#	Item	Crystal Iridescent	Forest Green	Sapphire Blue	Royal Ruby	White
6	Bowl, 4", berry	$4.00		$18.00		
5	Bowl, 4½", fruit, B1664	$4.50	$11.00	$14.00	$8.00	$4.50
1	Bowl, 5¼", cereal, B1665	$10.00	$20.00	$14.00		
20	Bowl, 6½", deep	$20.00				
7	Bowl, 7¾", flat soup, B1667	$12.00		$15.00		$15.00
11	Bowl, 8⅜", large berry, B1678	$10.00	$14.00	$16.50	$20.00	$10.00
	Bowl, 8½", shallow (pink $8.00; Jade-ite, Vitrock, $20.00)			$19.00		
	Bowl, 9", flanged (2 styles)			$450.00		
15	Candlesticks, pr. (black, $100.00)	$25.00	$125.00			
4	Creamer	$6.00	$12.00	$35.00		$6.50
9	Cup, #B1650	$3.50	$8.00	$4.00	$8.00	$5.00
	Lamp, three styles	$50.00				
19	Pitcher, 64 oz., ice lip	$125.00			$60.00	
12	Plate, 6¾", bread and butter, B1630	$3.00	$4.00	$4.00		$3.00
3	Plate, 9⅜", grill			$22.50		
13	Plate, 9⅜", dinner, B1614	$7.00	$22.00	$6.00	$24.00	$9.00
8	Platter, 12", oval, B1646	$12.00		$16.00		
10	Saucer, B1628	$1.00	$3.00	$1.00	$4.00	$2.00
16	Stem, 4½ oz., cocktail	$4.00	$12.50		$12.50	
18	Stem, 5½ oz., juice	$5.00	$14.00		$14.00	
2	Sugar	$6.00	$12.00	$25.00		$6.50
	Tidbit, 2 tier				$75.00	
17	Tumbler, 6 oz., juice	$3.50			$8.00	
	Tumbler, 8 oz., 3¼", old fashioned	$10.00				
21	Tumbler, 9 oz., water	$5.00			$9.00	
	Tumbler, 12 oz., 4½", iced tea	$12.00			$12.50	
14	Tumbler, 16 oz., 5⅞", lemonade	$15.00			$16.00	

*not Anchor Hocking

Patterns – *"Forget Me Not," "Blue & Gold Floral,"* 1964 – 1966

White with decals	
Bowl, 4⅜", dessert	$8.00
Bowl, 5", chili or cereal	$12.00
Bowl, 6⅝", soup plate	$20.00
Bowl, 8¼", vegetable	$22.00
6 Casserole, 1 qt., w/cover	$25.00
4 Casserole, 1½ qt., oval, w/cover	$25.00
Creamer	$10.00
Cup, 8 oz.	$7.50
3 Custard	$8.00
Loaf pan, 5" x 9"	$30.00
7 Loaf pan, 5" x 9", baking, with cover	$30.00
8 Mug, 8 oz.	$18.00
Plate, 10", dinner	$14.00
5 Platter, 9" x 12"	$22.00
2 Sugar	$12.00
1 Sugar lid	$5.00
Saucer, 5¾"	$2.50

Patterns – *Meadow Green,* Decoration #75, 1967 – 1977

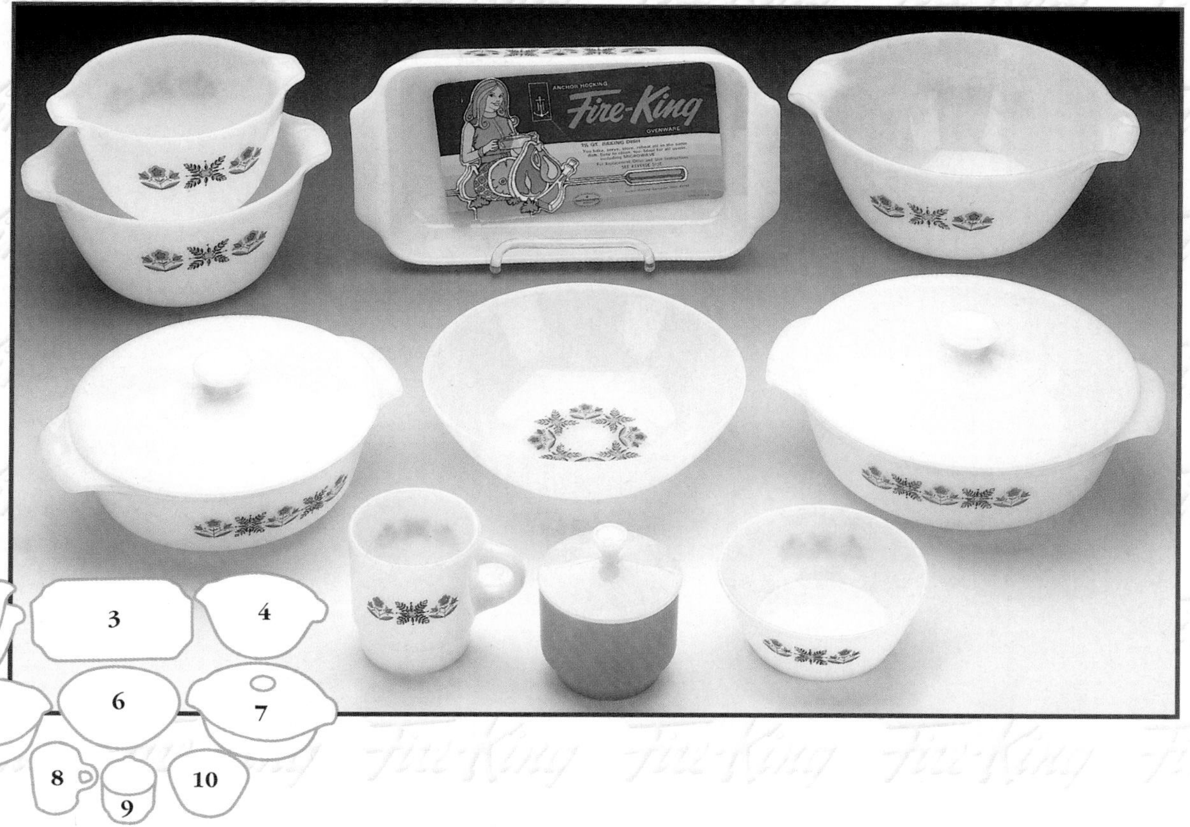

White with decals

Key	Item	Price
17	Bowl, 4⅝", dessert, W4674	$3.50
10	Bowl, 5", 8 oz., cereal, W310	$3.00
	Bowl, 6⅝", soup, W4667	$6.00
6	Bowl, 8¼", vegetable, W4678	$12.00
1	Bowl, 1½ qt., mixing	$6.00
2	Bowl, 2 qt., mixing	$8.00
4	Bowl, 2½ qt., mixing	$10.00
	Cake dish, 8", square, W435	$6.00
22	Cake dish, 9", round, W429	$6.50
19	Casserole, 12 oz., hdld., W240E	$3.50
	Casserole, 1 qt., w/knob cover, W436	$7.00
5	Casserole, 1½ qt., w/knob cover, W437	$8.00
21	Casserole, 1½ qt., oval, w/au gratin cover (smooth)	$10.00
7	Casserole, 2 qt., w/knob cover, W438	$9.00
	Casserole, 3 qt., w/knob cover, W439	$10.00
15	Creamer, two styles, W4644	$3.00
13	Cup, 7½ oz., W4659	$2.50
20	Custard, 6 oz., W434	$1.50
18	Loaf dish, 5" x 9", W441	$6.50
8	Mug, 8 oz., W312	$3.00
12	Plate, 7⅜", salad, W4638	$2.50
11	Plate, 10", dinner, W4646	$4.00
14	Platter, 12" x 9", W4647	$8.00
16	Saucer, W4649	$.50
9	Sugar w/lid, two colors, W4643	$7.00
	Utility baking dish, 1½ qt., W432	$6.00
3	Utility baking dish, 2 qt., W431	$7.00

W4600/85
16 Piece
DINNERWARE SET
Meadow Green Pattern
4 SAUCERS INSIDE

12

11

13

Patterns – *Meadow Green*

12
11
10
9
15
14
8
13
9
15
6
16
17

White with decals

	Item	Price
	Bowl, 4⅝", dessert	$3.50
	Bowl, 6⅝", soup plate	$9.00
	Bowl, 8¼", vegetable	$14.00
13	Cake pan, 8", round	$12.00
	Cake pan, 8", square	$12.00
10	Casserole, 1 pt., knob cover	$9.00
5	Casserole, 1 qt., knob cover	$12.00
12	Casserole, 1½ qt., knob cover	$12.00
9	Casserole, 1½ qt., oval, w/au gratin cover	$15.00
	Casserole, 2 qt., knob cover	$16.00
	Comport, 10", ftd., Vintage	$165.00
	Comport, 11", ftd., Lace Edge	$165.00
	Creamer	$5.00
	Cup, 5 oz., snack	$3.00
	Cup, 8 oz.	$3.00
6	Custard, 6 oz., low or dessert	$3.50
	Egg plate	$175.00
8	Gravy or sauce boat	$295.00
1	Mug	$95.00
	Pan, 5" x 9", baking, w/cover	$18.00
7	Pan, 5" x 9", deep loaf	$14.00
2	Pan, 6½" x 10½", utility baking	$12.00
12	Pan, 8" x 12½", utility baking	$35.00
	Plate, 7⅜", salad	$5.00
	Plate, 9⅛", dinner	$7.00
	Platter, 9" x 12"	$15.00
	Saucer, 5¾"	$1.00
4	Shaker, pr. (2 styles)	$325.00
	Sugar	$5.00
	Sugar cover	$5.00
	Tray, 11" x 6", rectangular, snack	$5.00
	Tumbler, 5 oz., juice (white)	$30.00
	Tumbler, 4⅛", 9½ oz., water (white)	$95.00
	Tumbler, 10 oz., water (crystal)	$50.00
3	Tumbler, 11 oz. (white)	$25.00
	Vase	$165.00

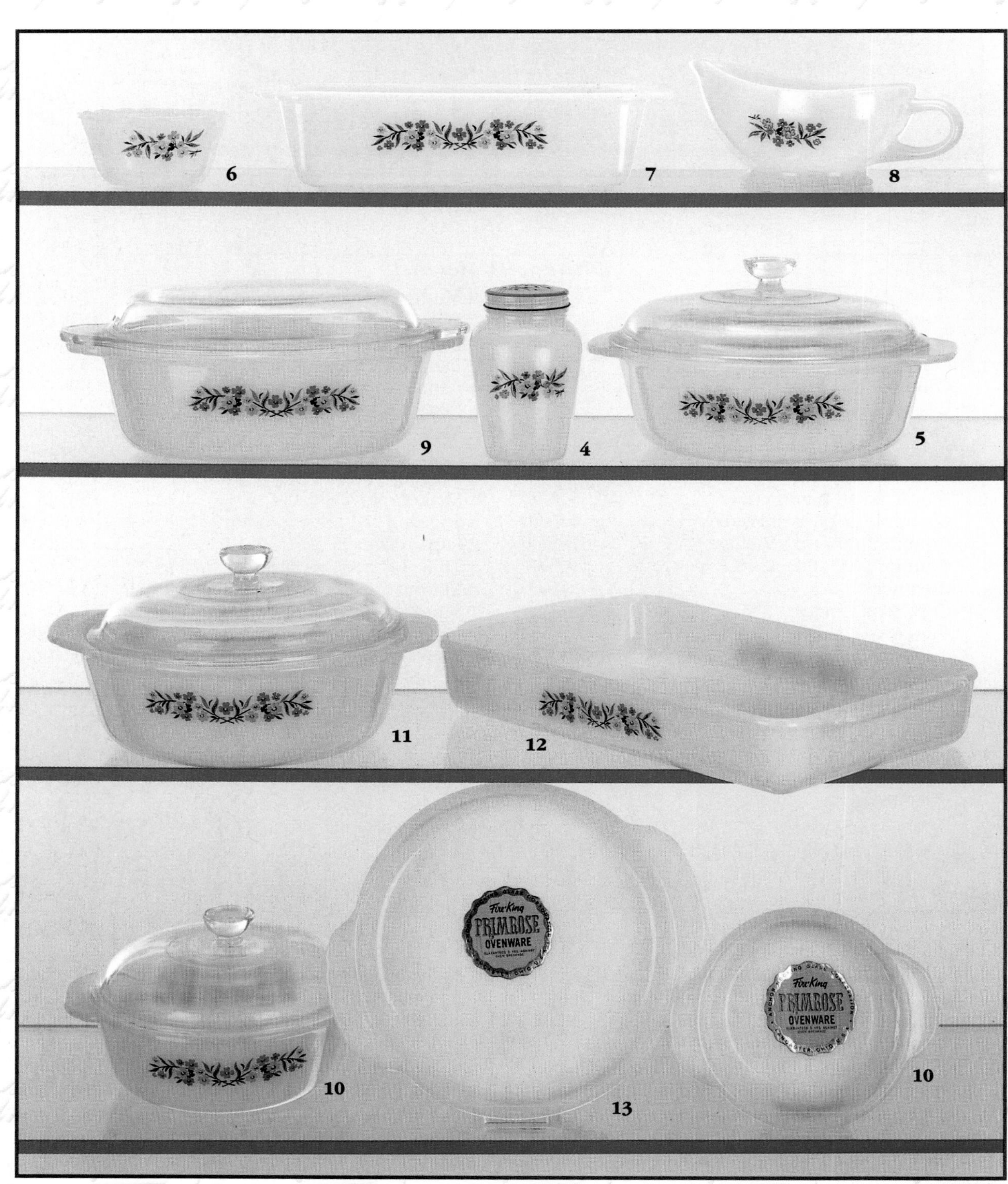
6
7
8
9
4
5
11
12
Fire-King
PRIMROSE
OVENWARE
Fire-King
PRIMROSE
OVENWARE
10
13
10

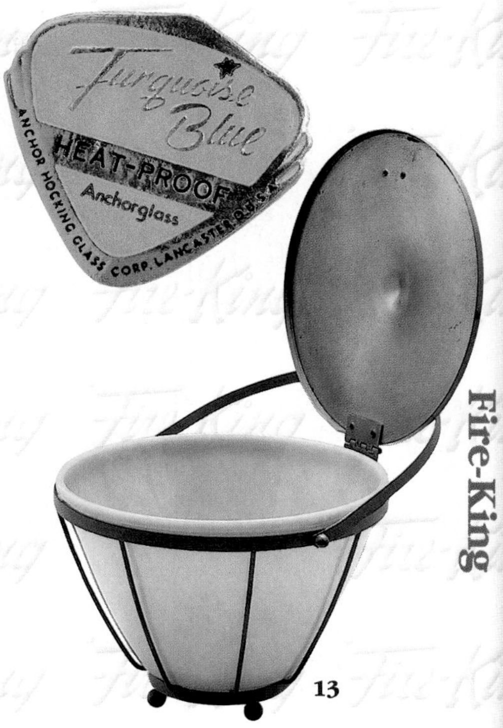

5	Bowl, 4½", berry $10.00	6	Cup, B4079 . . . .$5.00
15	Bowl, 5", cereal or chili, 2⅜" high, B291 . .$15.00	2	Mug, 8 oz., B1212 . . . .$10.00
8	Bowl, 5", cereal (thin), 2" high $48.00	12	Plate, 6⅛", bread and butter, B4037 . . . . .$18.00
4	Bowl, 5", "Davy Crockett" style $110.00	11	Plate, 7¼", salad, B4038 . . . .$12.00
17	Bowl, 6⅞", soup/salad, B4067 . . . .$25.00	10	Plate, 9", B4041 . . . .$12.00
16	Bowl, 8", vegetable, B4078 . . . .$23.00	14	Plate, 9", w/cup indent $6.00
13	Casserole/ice bucket, 2 qt., B367 . . . .$45.00	9	Plate, 10", B4046 . . . .$30.00
	with box $60.00	7	Saucer, B4029 . . . .$1.50
3	Creamer, B4054 . . . .$8.00	1	Sugar, B4053 . . . .$8.00

Patterns – *Wheat,* 1962 – 1966

Fire-King

White with decal

- 2 Bowl, 4⅝", dessert $3.50
- Bowl, 5", chili $30.00
- 13 Bowl, 6⅝", soup plate $8.00
- 9 Bowl, 8¼", vegetable $12.00
- Cake pan, 8", round $11.00
- Cake pan, 8", square $10.00
- Casserole, 1 pt., w/knob cover $8.00
- 14 Casserole, 1 qt., w/knob cover $10.00
- Casserole, 1½ qt., w/knob cover $11.00
- Casserole, 1½ qt., oval, w/au gratin cover $14.00
- Casserole, 2 qt., w/knob cover $15.00
- 12 Creamer $5.00
- 4 Cup, 5 oz., snack $3.00
- 5 Cup, 8 oz. $4.00
- 2 Custard, 6 oz., low or dessert $3.00
- Mug $60.00
- Pan, 5" x 9", baking, w/cover $16.00
- 17 Pan, 5" x 9", deep loaf $12.00
- 15 Pan, 6½" x 10½" x 1½", utility baking $12.00
- 16 Pan, 8" x 12½" x 2", utility baking $18.00
- 7 Plate, 7⅞", salad $8.00
- 8 Plate, 10", dinner $6.00
- Platter, 9" x 12" $15.00
- 6 Saucer, 5¾" $1.00
- 10 Sugar $4.50
- 11 Sugar cover $5.00
- Tumbler, 5 oz., juice $6.00
- Tumbler, 11 oz., tea $8.00
- 3 Tray, 11" x 6", rectangular, snack $4.00

wheat dinnerware

Heat-resistant; golden wheat on a clean contemporary shape. Matches Wheat ovenware. In open stock and packaged sets.

			Doz. Ctn.	Lbs. Ctn.
W4679/65	8 oz	cup	3	14
W4629/65	5¾″	saucer	3	14
W4674/65	4⅝″	dessert	3	11
W4638/65	7⅜″	salad plate	3	23
W4667/65	6⅝″	soup plate	3	25
W4646/65	10″	dinner plate	3	44
W4678/65	8¼″	vegetable bowl	1	14
W4647/65	12 x 9″	platter	1	20
W4653/65		sugar/cover	1	9
W4654/65		creamer	1	7

Packed Sets		Sets Ctn.	Lbs. Ctn.
W4600/46	16 pc set, display carton, 4 cups, 4 saucers, 4 desserts, 4 dinner plates	4	38
W4600/47	35 pc set, 6 cups, 6 saucers, 6 desserts, 6 soup plates, 6 dinner plates, vegetable, platter, sugar/cover, creamer	1	23
W4600/48	53 pc set, 8 cups, 8 saucers, 8 desserts, 8 salad plates, 8 soup plates, 8 dinner plates, vegetable, platter, sugar/cover, creamer	1	34

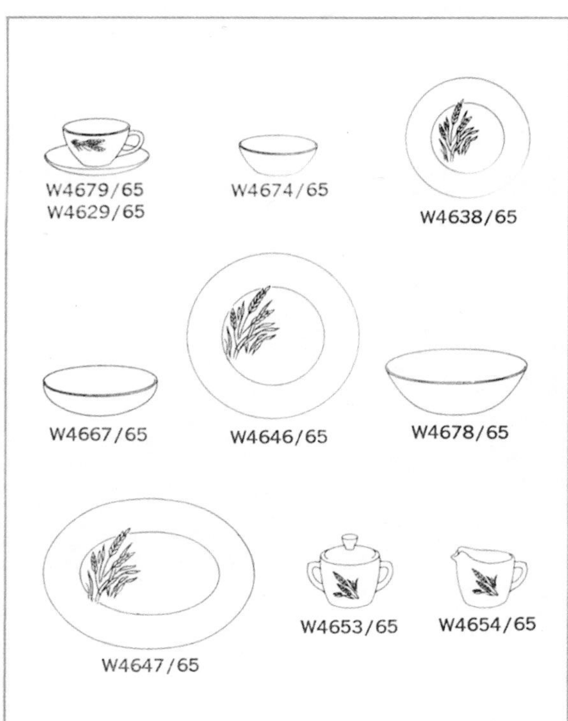

Items – *Bowls, Mixing, Swedish Modern*

Top row: All 5"
Middle/bottom rows: 8⅜", 7¼", 6", 5"

	5"	6"	7¼"	8⅜"
Anchorwhite	$15.00			
Jade-ite	$55.00	$125.00	$100.00	$125.00
Turquoise Blue	$30.00	$35.00	$35.00	$60.00

Items – *Bowls, Mixing, Swirl*

G4156, 6"
G4157, 7"
G4158, 8"
G4159, 9"
Jade-ite
(priced on p. 53)

7", 8", 9"
Peach Luster
(priced on p. 53)

	5"	6"	7"	8"	9"
Anchorwhite	$20.00	$5.00	$7.50	$7.50	$12.00
Ivory, #4100 heat resisting		$7.50	$10.00	$12.50	$15.00
Jade-ite	$165.00	$28.00	$25.00	$28.00	$30.00
Peach Luster		$10.00	$10.00	$12.50	$15.00
Rainbow		$22.00	$26.00	$26.00	$26.00

Top row:
7", 8", 9" Jade-ite
7", 8", 9" Rainbow
Bottom row:
7", 8", 9" Ivory
5" Jade-ite
6", 7", 8", 9" Peach Luster

6" Peach Luster, 6" Jade-ite, 5" Ivory

6", 7", 8", 9" Rainbow

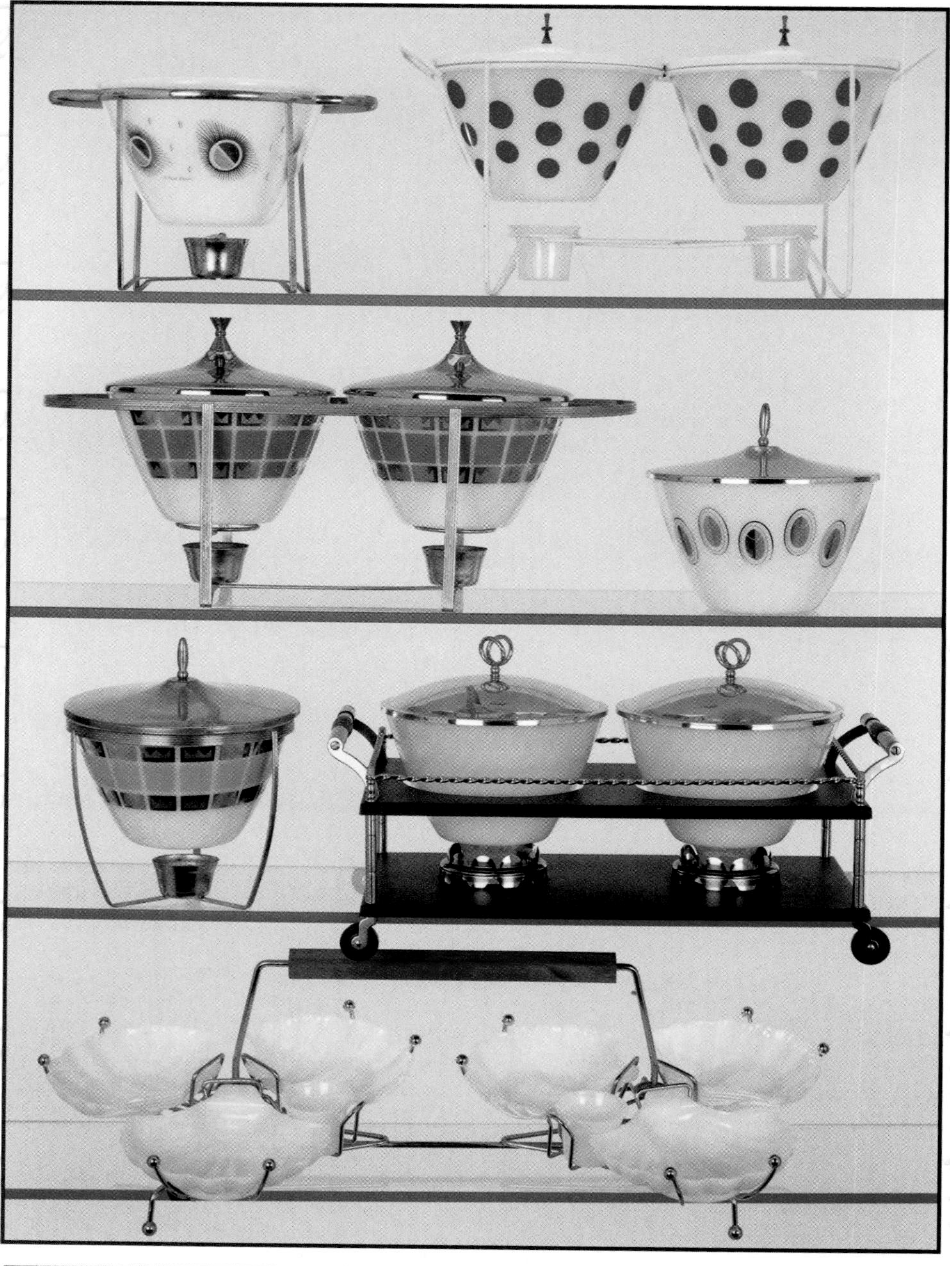

2-qt. Splash Proof bowls unless noted

Row 1:

Fred Press decorated, W300 .... $20.00

Double Red Dots #182, W300, w/glass votive candle holders, signed "Fire-King" $50.00

Row 2:

Double Fred Press $40.00

Fred Press, w/lid only $17.50

Row 3:

Fred Press $20.00

Double white, w/fancy cart $35.00

Row 4:

Six Sea Shell, w/glass votive candle holders, signed "Fire-King" $40.00

Row 1:

Super Fruit;
pear, apple, orange, lemon ......$5.00 each
Smiling apple $6.00
Foxy Flowers; yellow, red ....$5.00 each

Row 2:

Strawberry Shortcake $10.00
Raspberry Tart $10.00
Ziggy, coffee, "Black" $12.00
Fruits, signed "Nancy Lyon" (?);
lemon, plum, strawberry, assorted . .$12.00 each

Row 3:

Apple Dumplin' $10.00
Blueberry Pie $10.00
Ziggy, coffee, "Cream and Sugar" $12.00
Birds; Toucan, Cockatoo,
Parrot, Bird of Paradise ....$10.00 each

Row 4:

Snoopy (1 – 4) ....$12.00 each
Pastoral scene $4.00
Holly Hobbie and Robby $12.00
Norwegian witch $15.00

Row 5:

Snoopy $12.00
Snoopy $12.00
Snoopy for President .$17.50
Snoopy for President .$17.50
Snoopy $12.00
Snoopy Christmas $17.50
Snoopy $12.00

Honeymoon Hideaway, $8.00

Row 1:
- Tulsa Experimental Aircraft Association $20.00
- Tom and Jerry, the Beverage Mart $6.00
- Fired-on; blue, yellow . . . . $5.00 each
- Ivory w/pink elephant decals . . . . $15.00 each
- Spot restaurant, Piqua/Sidney, Ohio $3.00

Row 2:
- Old car $6.00
- Ohio School Pictures $3.00
- Rio Grande Railroad $25.00
- Rorschach test? $4.00
- Indiana Pacers $10.00
- Shamrocks $8.00
- Sheep dog $10.00

Row 3:
- Ozark Firewater, Peach Lustre $12.00
- White Castle white cola $15.00
- Ranger, Nugget Yellow $5.00
- "Lindbergh in Paris" headline $15.00
- Consumers Co-op Oil Company $3.00
- Concord, blue $3.00
- America's Bicentennial $6.00

Row 4:
- State Bank of Kingsland
  Consumers Co-op Oil $3.00
- Morocco order $3.00
- Ditch Witch $3.00
- "Texas" $5.00
- Pillsbury $12.00
- Kansas City Royals $10.00
- State Bank of Kingsland
  Consumers Co-op Oil $3.00

Row 5:
- Blue Willow $10.00
- Rainbow $4.00
- Captain Crunch $25.00
- Floral $3.00
- Gibson Girl $20.00
- Hillbilly shanty $6.00
- Jeans $6.00

Row 1:

Camelot mug $3.00
Camelot mug $3.00
Kimberly mug $4.00
Camelot mug $3.00
Kimberly mug $4.00
Spruce Goose $25.00
R.M.S. Queen Mary $12.50

Row 2:

Gingham;
green, red, yellow, blue $5.00
Chicago Cubs $25.00
Chicago $12.50
McDonald's ("Many Happy Returns") . .$10.00 each

Row 3:

Butterflies $6.00
Signed "Hildi";
mouse, frog, love bugs, caterpillar . .$10.00 each

Row 4:

Burger Queen $15.00
Super Stripe;
orange, green, blue . . . .$4.00 each
Pop Floral;
rose, tulip, violet . . . .$5.00 each

Row 5:

Bazooka bubble gum $100.00
A & W $15.00
Stuckey's coffee club .$12.00
Bonanza $15.00
Burger Chef $15.00
Burger King $15.00
McDonald's $5.00

Christmas mug, $30.00

Ovenware Patterns – *"Blue Heaven,"* 1970s

Anchorwhite with decal	
Bowl, 5", chili $12.00	Casserole, 1 qt., w/crystal knob cover . . . $12.00
6 Bowl, 1 qt., mixing $15.00	Casserole, 1½ qt., oval w/au gratin cover . $22.50
7 Bowl, 1½ qt., mixing $20.00	9 Casserole, 1½ qt., w/crystal knob cover . . $20.00
3 Bowl, 2½ qt., mixing $20.00	Casserole, 2 qt., w/crystal knob cover . . . $22.50
Cake pan, 8", square $10.00	10 Custard, 6 oz. $4.00
4 Cake pan, 8", round $10.00	2 Loaf pan, 5" x 9", deep $10.00
1 Casserole, 12 oz., hdld. $15.00	5 Mug, 8 oz. $12.00
Casserole, 1 pt. $12.00	8 Utility dish, 6½" x 10½" $8.00

Ovenware Patterns – *Candle Glow*, *Decoration #73, 1967 – 1972*

Original lids for casseroles were rather flat milk white with a flat top knob.

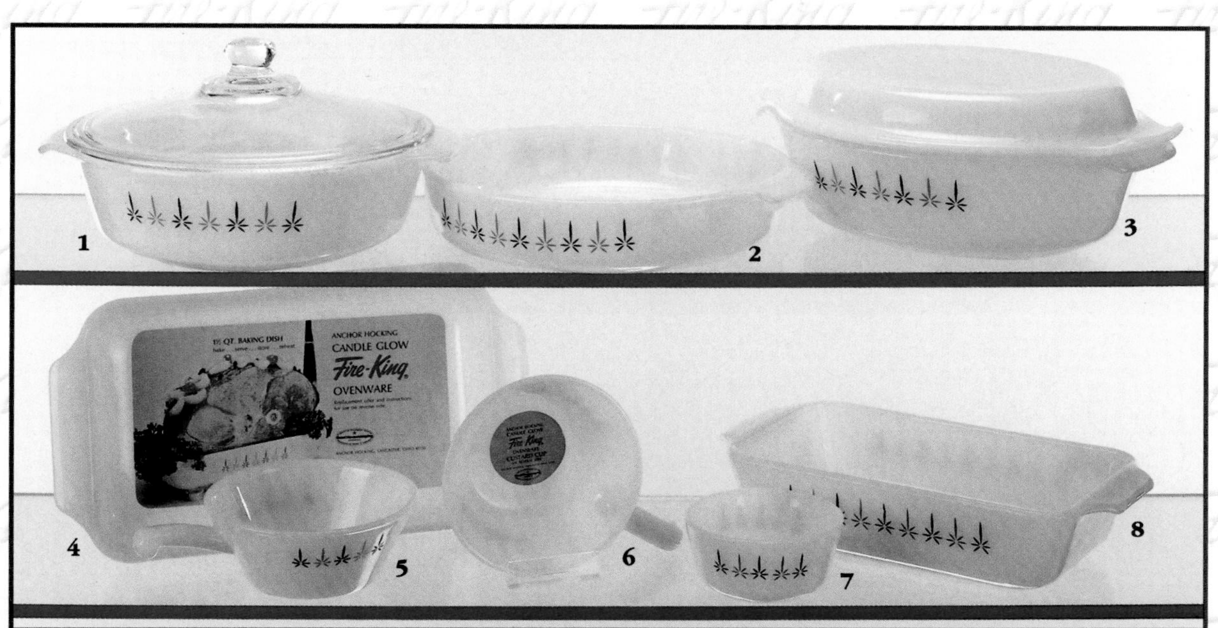

Anchorwhite with decal

- (5) Bowl, 5", 8 oz., cereal, W310 . . . .$5.00
- (9) Bowl, 1 qt., mixing, set W600 . . . .$10.00
- (10) Bowl, 1½ qt., mixing, set W600 . . . .$12.00
- (11) Bowl, 2½ qt., mixing, set W600 . . . .$14.00
- Cake dish, 8", square, W435 . . . .$7.00
- (2) Cake dish, 9", round, W429 . . . .$7.50
- (6) Casserole, 12 oz., hdld., #240 . . . .$4.50
- Casserole, 1 pt. $10.00
- (1) Casserole, 1 qt., w/white cover, #436 . . . .$9.00
- Casserole, 1½ qt., w/white cover, #437 . . .$10.00
- (3) Casserole, 1½ qt., oval, w/white augratin cover, #433 . . . .$10.00
- Casserole, 2 qt., w/white cover, #438 . . . .$12.00
- Casserole, 3 qt., w/white cover, #439 . . . .$16.00
- (7) Custard, 6 oz., W434 . . . .$2.00
- (8) Loaf pan, 5" x 9", W441 . . . .$7.50
- Mug, 8 oz., stacking, W312 . . . .$7.00
- (4) Utility dish, 1½ qt., W432 . . . .$6.00
- Utility dish, 2 qt., W431 . . . .$12.00

Ovenware Patterns – *Chanticleer or Country Kitchen,* 1965 – 1967

Anchorwhite with decal

No.	Item	Price
1	Bowl, 5", chili	$12.00
11	Bowl, 1 qt., mixing, W600	$18.00
10	Bowl, 1½ qt., mixing, W600	$22.00
9	Bowl, 2½ qt., mixing, W600	$22.00
8	Bowl, 3½ qt., mixing, W600	$30.00
	Cake pan, 8", square	$10.00
4	Cake pan, 8", round	$10.00
3	Casserole, 12 oz., hdld.	$18.00
	Casserole, 1 pt.	$12.00
	Casserole, 1 qt., w/crystal knob cover	$12.00
	Casserole, 1½ qt., oval, w/au gratin cover	$22.50
7	Casserole, 1½ qt., w/crystal knob cover	$20.00
	Casserole, 2 qt., w/crystal knob cover	$22.50
13	Cup, snack	$15.00
5	Custard, 6 oz.	$4.00
2	Loaf pan, 5" x 9", deep	$10.00
6	Mug, 8 oz.	$20.00
12	Utility dish, 6½" x 10½"	$8.00
	Utility dish, 8" x 12½"	$22.00

Baker, 1½ qt., no cover $6.50	12 Casserole, 1½ qt., oval, w/au gratin cover (smooth) $10.00
Baking pan and cover, 5" x 9", L469 . . . .$10.00	10 Casserole, 2 qt., w/crystal or white knob cover, L408 . . . . .$10.00
7 Bowl, 5", "Danish Swirl" $6.00	5 Custard, 6 oz., plain or scalloped rim, L424 . . .$3.00
Cake pan, 8", square, L452 . . . .$7.00	1 Custard, 6 oz., "Danish Swirl" $4.00
9 Cake pan, 8", round, L450 . . . .$7.00	Dish, 11¾", divided, oval, L468 . . . .$6.00
Casserole, 10 oz., "Danish Swirl" $7.00	6 Loaf pan, 5" x 9", deep, L409 . . . .$8.00
3 Casserole, 12 oz., French handled, w/cover, L235 . . . .$5.00	2 Pie, 5⅜", individual, "Danish Swirl" $5.00
Casserole, 1 pt., w/crystal or white cover, L405 . .$7.00	Pie plate, 9", L460 . . . .$5.00
Casserole, 1 qt., w/crystal or white knob cover, L406 . . . .$8.00	Pie plate, 10" $6.00
Casserole, 1½ qt., w/crystal or white knob cover, L407 . . . .$8.00	8 Utility baking pan, 6½" x 10½", L410 . . . .$8.00
	Utility baking pan, 8" x 12½", L411 . . . .$9.00

CRYSTAL *Fire-King*® OVENWARE — GUARANTEED

H422

H423

H424

	PACKING
H422—5 oz. Standard Custard	6 doz. — 19 lbs.
H423—6 oz. Egg Cup & Deep Custard	4 doz. — 15 lbs.
H424—6 oz. Dessert or Low Custard	4 doz. — 15 lbs.

H425

H426

H402

H425—10 oz. Deep Pie Dish	3 doz. — 18 lbs.
H426—15 oz. Deep Pie Dish	3 doz. — 21 lbs.
H402— 8 oz. Individual Casserole & Cover	2 doz. — 20 lbs.

H405 — H406

H407 — H408

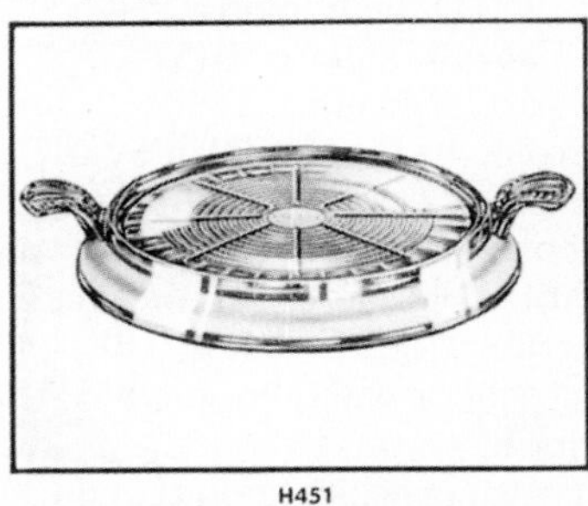

H451

H405—1 Pt. Casserole—Knob Cover	1 doz. — 17 lbs.
H406—1 Qt. Casserole—Knob Cover	½ doz. — 14 lbs.
H407—1 ½ Qt. Casserole—Knob Cover	½ doz. — 19 lbs.
H408—2 Qt. Casserole—Knob Cover	½ doz. — 21 lbs.
H451— Table Server	1 doz. — 15 lbs.

H497

H467

H449

H497—1 ½ Qt. Casseorle—Utility Cover	½ doz. — 19 lbs.
H467—1 ½ Qt. Oval Casserole—Au Gratin Cover	½ doz. — 18 lbs.
H449—3 Qt. Double Roaster (2 Pce. Unit) (Each in Gift Carton)	1/3 doz. — 31 lbs.

HEAT-PROOF

SEE GUARANTEE ON PAGE 8.

CRYSTAL *Fire-King*® OVENWARE — GUARANTEED

H450

H452

H443

		PACKING
H450—8"	Round Cake Pan	½ doz. — 12 lbs.
H452—8"	Square Cake Pan	½ doz. — 18 lbs.
H443—1 Qt.	Pudding Pan	1 doz. — 15 lbs.

H409

H469

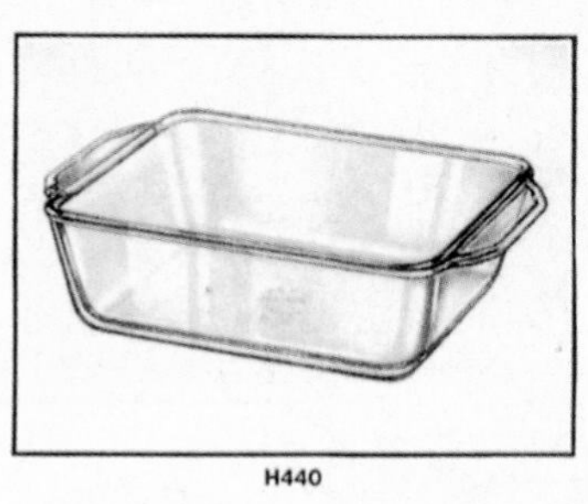
H440

H409—5 x 9"	Deep Loaf Pan	½ doz. — 12 lbs.
H469—5 x 9"	Baking Pan & Cover	½ doz. — 19 lbs.
H440—6¼ x 7¼"	Square Baking Pan	½ doz. — 11 lbs.

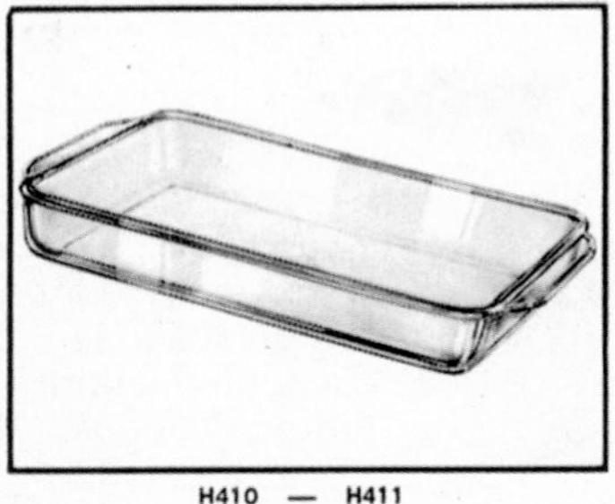
H410 — H411

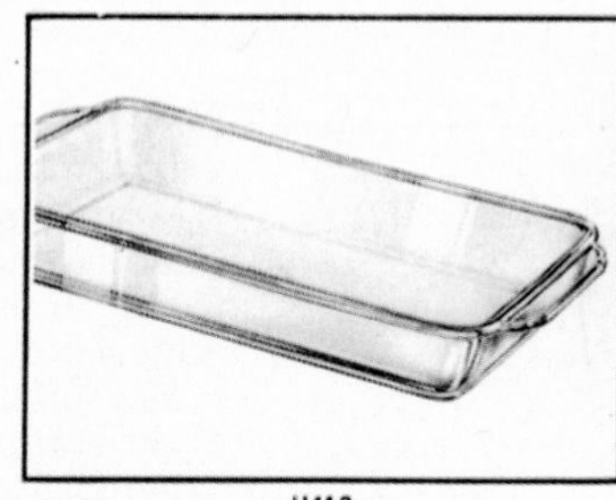
H412

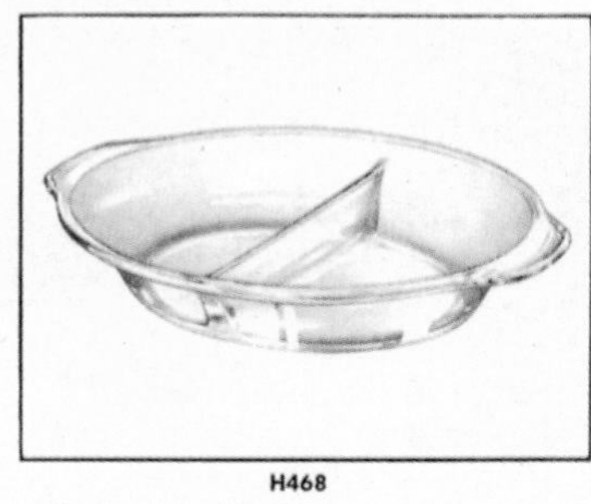
H468

H410— 6½ x 10½"	Utility Baking Pan (1½ Qt.)	½ doz. — 15 lbs.
H411— 8 x 12½"	Utility Baking Pan (2 Qt.)	½ doz. — 23 lbs.
H412— 9½ x 14⅛"	Utility Baking Pan (3 Qt.)	½ doz. — 29 lbs.
H468—11¾"	Oval Divided Dish	½ doz. — 14 lbs.

H496

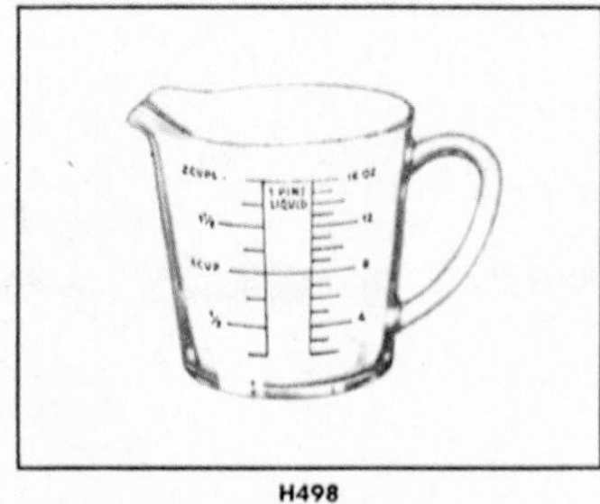
H498

H499

H496— 8 oz.	Measuring Cup—Black Graduations	1 doz. — 8 lbs.
H498—16 oz.	Measuring Pitcher—Black Graduations	1 doz. — 13 lbs.
H499— 1 Qt.	Measuring Pitcher—Black Graduations	½ doz. — 12 lbs.

SEE GUARANTEE ON PAGE 8.

Continued on Pages 8 and 9.

Ovenware Patterns – *Crystal,* 1947 – 1992

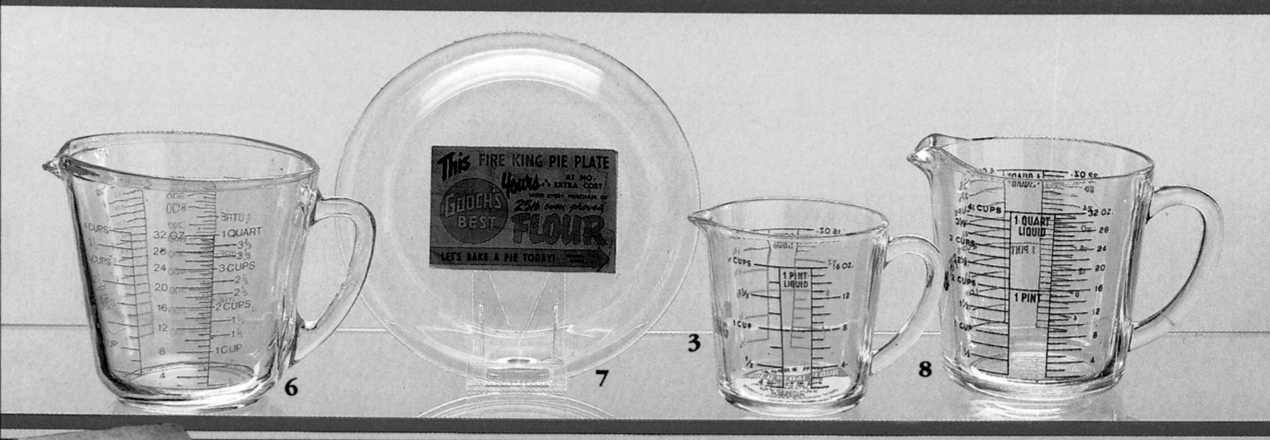

Baker, 8 oz., no cover $3.00
2 Baker, 1 qt., no cover $3.50
Baker, 1½ qt., no cover $3.50
4 Baker, 2 qt., no cover $4.00
Baking pan, 5" x 9", w/cover $9.00
Baking pan, 6¼" x 7¼", square $6.00
Cake pan, 8", round $7.00
Cake pan, 8", square $7.00
Casserole, 8 oz. w/crystal knob cover $4.00
Casserole, 1 pt., w/crystal knob cover $4.00
Casserole, 1 qt., w/crystal knob cover $5.00
Casserole, 1½ qt., w/crystal knob cover $6.00
Casserole, 1½ qt., w/utility cover $6.00
Casserole, 1½ qt., oval, w/au gratin cover . . .$7.00
12 Casserole, 2 qt., w/crystal knob cover $8.00
Casserole, 3 qt., double roaster $18.00
15 Custard, 5 oz. $2.00
Custard, 6 oz., deep $2.50
Custard, 6 oz., low $2.50
Dish, 11¾", oval, divided $5.00
13 Loaf pan, 5" x 9" $7.00
1 Measuring cup, 8 oz., black graduations $6.00
Measuring cup, 8 oz., red graduations $4.00
5 Measuring pitcher, 16 oz., black graduations $12.00
3 Measuring pitcher, 16 oz., red graduations . .$8.00
6 Measuring pitcher, 32 oz., black graduations $15.00
8 Measuring pitcher, 32 oz., red graduations . .$10.00
Percolator top $2.50
7 Pie dish, 10 oz., deep $3.00
Pie dish, 15 oz., deep $3.50
10 Pie pan, 8" $4.00
9 Pie pan, 9" $5.00
11 Pie pan, 9", deep dish $10.00
16 Pudding pan, 1 qt. $4.00
Table server $10.00
14 Utility dish, 6½" x 10½" $5.00
Utility dish, 8" x 12½" $6.00
Utility dish, 9½" x 14⅛" $7.00

Anchorwhite with decal

#	Item	Price
3	Bowl, 5", chili	$10.00
8	Bowl, 1 qt., mixing	$15.00
9	Bowl, 1½ qt., mixing	$20.00
7	Bowl, 2½ qt., mixing	$20.00
	Cake pan, 8", square	$15.00
	Cake pan, 8", round	$15.00
	Casserole, 12 oz., hdld.	$15.00
	Casserole, 1 pt.	$12.00
	Casserole, 1 qt., w/crystal knob cover	$12.00
	Casserole, 1½ qt., oval, w/au gratin cover	$22.50
	Casserole, 1½ qt., w/crystal knob cover	$20.00
	Casserole, 2 qt., w/crystal knob cover	$22.50
5	Custard, 6 oz.	$5.00
2	Loaf pan, deep, 5" x 9"	$10.00
1	Mug, 8 oz.	$10.00
4	Utility dish, 6½" x 10½"	$15.00

Hand-decorated red Distlefink Anchorwhite and Ivory

Row 1:
- Refrigerator container, 4" x 8" $70.00
- Casserole, 2 qt. $80.00
- Casserole, 1 pt. $65.00

Row 2:
- Casserole, 1½ qt., oval, w/au gratin lid . . .$85.00
- Bowl, 8¾", mixing $125.00
- Refrigerator container, 4" x 4" $50.00

Row 3:
- Baking pan, 6½" x 10½" $75.00
- Loaf, 5" x 9", deep $85.00

Hand-decorated Anchorwhite and Ivory

Row 1:

Item	Price
Baking pan, 6½" x 10½", "Yellow Rose"	$65.00
Loaf, 5" x 9", deep, "Yellow Rose"	$60.00
Casserole, 1 pt., "Pine Cone"	$45.00
Casserole, 1 pt., "Yellow Rose"	$60.00

Row 2:

Item	Price
Casserole, 1½ qt., oval, "Ivy," w/au gratin lid	$70.00
Bowl, 1 qt., mixing, "Ivy"	$50.00
Bowl, 1½ qt., mixing, "Ivy"	$50.00
Casserole, 1 qt., "Ivy"	$55.00

Ovenware Patterns – *"Peach Blossom"*

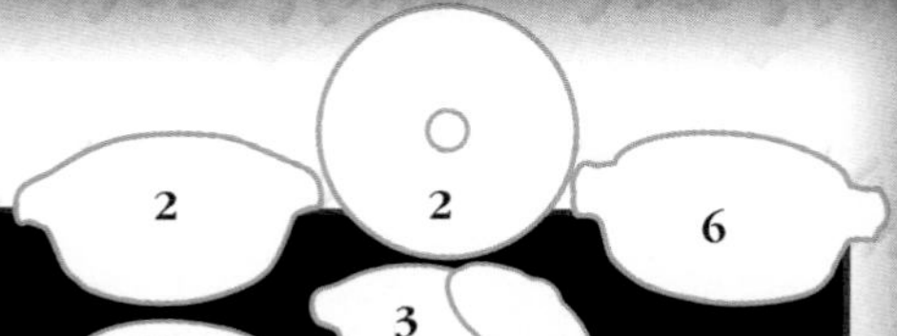

- 24 Baking pan, 6½" x 10½" $30.00
- 12 Bowl, 2 qt., mixing, w/gold leaf, Federal .$20.00
- 11 Bowl, 3 qt., mixing, w/gold leaf, Federal .$20.00
- 17 Bowl, 5", chili $12.00
- 21 Bowl, 6", mixing, Colonial Kitchen $16.00
- 14 Bowl, 7³⁄₁₆", mixing, Colonial Kitchen $18.00
- 19 Bowl, 8¾", mixing, Colonial Kitchen $20.00
- 4 Casserole, 12 oz., French handled $20.00
- 3 Casserole, 1 pt. $30.00
- 8 Casserole, 1 qt. $30.00
- 1 Casserole, 1 qt., tab handles, w/white lid . .$45.00
- 13 Casserole, 1½ qt. $25.00
- 16 Casserole, 1½ qt., oval, w/au gratin lid . . .$30.00
- 6 Casserole, 1½ qt., oval, w/au gratin white lid $45.00
- 2 Casserole, 2 qt. $30.00
- 18 Custard, 5 oz. $8.00
- 20 Custard, 6 oz. $8.00
- 7 Loaf pan, 5" x 9", deep $25.00
- 22 Mug, 8 oz. $12.00
- 15 Pan, cake, 8" x 8", square $30.00
- 5 Refrigerator, 4" x 4", square $15.00
- 10 Refrigerator, 4" x 8", rectangular $18.00
- 23 Refrigerator, 4¼", round, "star burst" lid . .$25.00
- 9 Refrigerator, 4¼" x 9", oval, "star burst" lid .$35.00

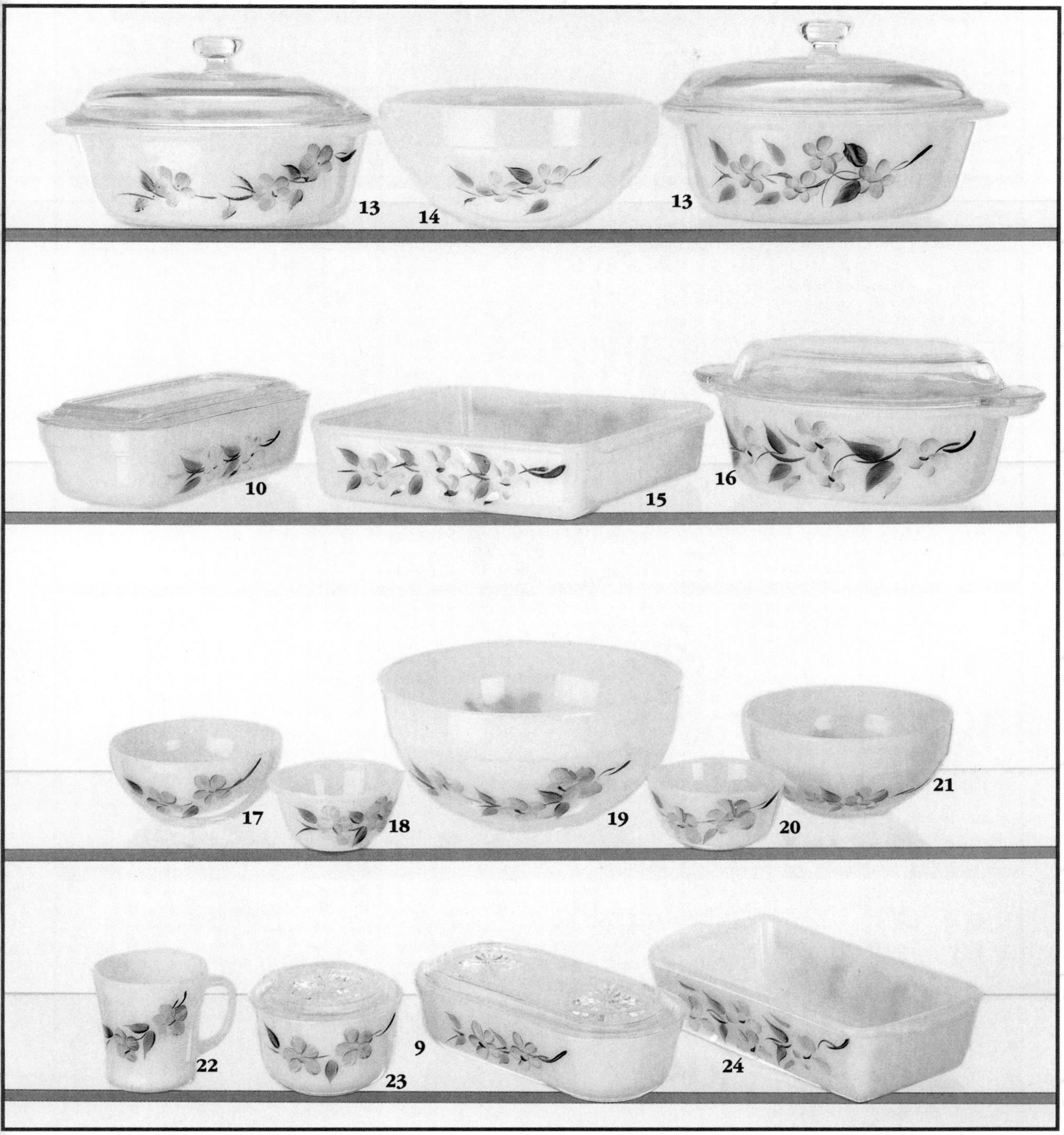

13 14 13

10 15 16

17 18 19 20 21

22 23 9 24

Ovenware Patterns – *Ivory and Ivory White,* 1948 – mid-1950s

Individual baker, 6 oz.

7 8 2

"Sweetheart Set"
12 pieces:
#407 Casserole and cover
#421 Bakers (6)
#410 Baking pan
#409 Deep Loaf pan
#450 Cake pan
#460 Pie pan

1 2 3 4 5 6

Row 1:
Pie dish, 5⅜", individual, deep, #465 . . . .$15.00
7 Casserole, 2 qt., w/knob cover, #408 . . . .$25.00
Same, with decal decoration #253 . . . . . .$60.00
Lid only, embossed "Fire-King" $22.50
Table server, #451 . . . .$17.50
Casserole, 1 pt. $30.00
Same, Ivory White $10.00

Row 2:
2 Pie pan, 9", #460 . . . .$10.00
Same, Ivory White $8.00
Pie pan, 8", Ivory White $22.50
3 Dessert, 5 oz., #421 . . . .$5.00
5 Cake pan, 9", round, #450 . . . .$15.00

Row 3:
8 Custard cup, 6 oz., deep $6.00
Baker, 6 oz., individual, #420 . . . .$5.00
1 Casserole, 1½ qt., #407 . . . .$20.00
6 Baking pan, 6½" x 10½", #410 . . . .$18.00

Row 4:
Casserole, 1 qt., pie plate lid (emb. Fire-King "Philbe" design) $150.00
Casserole, 1 qt. $27.50
Same, Ivory White $10.00
4 Loaf pan, 9⅝", deep, #409 . . . .$15.00

Ovenware Patterns – *Jade-ite,* *1945 – mid-1950s*

Row 1:

- Custard, 3⅝" x 1 9/16", ribbed, deep $125.00
- Custard, 3⅝" x 1⅝" deep $100.00
- Casserole, 7", Swirled . . . . morgue
- Baker, 5" x 1½", deep $110.00
- Casserole, 1½ qt. $2,250.00

Row 2:

- Skillet, 7", 2 spout $135.00
- Custard, 6 oz., individual $65.00
  - Set of six in wire holder $420.00
- 4½" x 5" jar
  (catalog description; lid, $20.00) $35.00

Row 3:

- Skillet, 7", 1 spout $65.00
- Pie plate, 9" $175.00
- Loaf pan, 5" x 9" $40.00

Ovenware Patterns – *Nature's Bounty,* 1976 – 1978

Anchorwhite with decal

	Item	Price
	Bowl, mixing, 1 qt.	$10.00
10	Bowl, mixing, 1½ qt.	$12.00
9	Bowl, mixing, 2½ qt.	$15.00
	Bowl, mixing, 3½ qt.	$18.00
12	Cake pan, 8", square	$10.00
5	Cake pan, 8", round	$10.00
	Casserole, 1 pt.	$12.50
4	Casserole, 1 qt., w/crystal knob cover	$12.00
8	Casserole, 1 qt., w/white lid	$14.00
11	Casserole, 1½ qt., oval, w/au gratin cover	$15.00
	Casserole, 1½ qt., w/crystal knob cover	$15.00
	Casserole, 2 qt., w/crystal knob cover	$15.00
	Casserole, 3 qt., w/crystal knob cover	$18.00
6	Custard, 6 oz.	$4.00
2	Loaf pan, deep, 5" x 9"	$10.00
1	Loaf pan, lid	$20.00
7	Mug, 8 oz.	$6.00
3	Utility dish, 6½" x 10½"	$10.00
	Utility dish, 8" x 12½"	$12.00

Ovenware Patterns – *Sapphire Blue, 1941 – 1956*

Baker, 1 pt., 4½" x 5", B3445 . . . .$8.00
Baker, 1 pt., 5⅝", round $8.00
Baker, 1 qt., 7¼", round, B3446 . . . .$12.00
Baker, 1½ qt., 8¼", round, B3447 . . . .$16.00
Baker, 2 qt., 8⅞", round, B3448 . . . .$16.00
Bowl, 4⅜", individual pie plate, #3457 . . .$22.00
8 Bowl, 4⅝", 2" high, three bands . . . . . . .morgue
Bowl, 5⅜", cereal or
deep-dish pie plate, #3465 . . . .$22.00
Bowl, 5 7/16", 2 11/16" deep (Kroger 12/30/44) .$400.00
Bowl, measuring-mixing, 16 oz. $27.50
Cake pan, 8¾", no tabs $45.00
Casserole, 10 oz., 4¾", individual $13.00
23 Casserole, 1 pt., 5⅝", w/knob cover, B3405 .$14.00
Casserole, 1 qt., 7¼", w/knob cover, #3406 $18.00
28 Casserole, 1 qt., pie plate cover $18.00
Casserole, 1½ qt., 8¼", w/knob cover, #3407 .$22.00
9 Casserole, 1½ qt., pie plate cover $20.00
1 Casserole, 2 qt., 8⅞", w/knob cover, #3408 . .$22.00
Casserole, 2 qt., pie plate cover $25.00
12 Cup, 8 oz., dry measure, no spout . . .$1,000.00
14 Cup, 8 oz., measuring, 1 spout, #897 . . . .$22.00
16 Cup, 8 oz., measuring, 3 spout $30.00
4 Custard cup or baker, 5 oz., B3420 . . . . . .$5.00
21 Custard cup or baker, 6 oz. (no design) . .$15.00
Custard cup or baker, 6 oz., shallow, B3421 . .$5.00
10 Custard cup or baker, 6 oz., 3⅜" deep, #3413 .$6.00
20 Custard cup or baker, 12 oz., 4 1/16" deep . .$400.00
19 Custard cup lid for 12 oz. (12/44) . . . . .morgue
18 Custard cup or baker,
19½ oz., 4¾" deep $450.00
Loaf pan, 9⅛" x 5⅛", deep, B3409 . . . .$22.00

17 Funnel . . . . .morgue
13 Mug, 7 oz., coffee, thick $28.00
Mug, 7 oz., coffee, thin $45.00
25 Nipple cover $265.00
15 Nurser, 4 oz., B3464 . . . .$20.00
24 Nurser, 8 oz., B3468 . . . .$35.00
Nurser, 8 oz., Fyrock $40.00
Nurser, 8 oz., "Tuffy"
Heatproof/Coldproof $35.00
22 Percolator top, 2⅛", B5 . . . .$5.00
27 Pie plate, 8⅜", 1½" deep, B3459 . . . .$9.00
3 Pie plate, 9", 1½" deep, B3460 . . . .$10.00
Pie plate, 9⅝", 1½" deep, B3461 . . . .$10.00
26 Pie plate, 10⅜", juice saver, B3462 . . . . .$150.00
Popcorn popper $40.00
Refrigerator jar & cover, 4½" x 5", B3494 .$15.00
Refrigerator jar & cover, 5⅛" x 9⅛", B3499 .$32.50
30 Roaster, 8¾", B3450 . . . .$55.00
29 Roaster, 10⅜", B3449 . . . .$80.00
5 Skillet, 7", w/4⅝" handle $1,000.00
Silex, 2-cup dripolator
(without insert, $20.00) $40.00
Silex, 6-cup coffee dripolator $225.00
2 Table server,
tab handles (w/design), B3451 . . . . . .$22.00
Table server, tab handles (no design) . . .$70.00
11 Utility bowl, 6⅞", 1 qt. $18.00
Utility bowl, 8⅜", 1½ qt. $20.00
7 Utility bowl, 10⅛", 2 qt. $22.00
Utility pan, 8⅛" x 12½", B3411 . . . .$100.00
6 Utility pan, 10½" x 2" deep, B3410 . . . . . .$25.00

12
13
14
15
16
17
18
19
20
20
21
22
23
24
25
26
27
FIRE-KING
OVEN-GLASS
28
29
30

FIRE - KING OVEN GLASS

Housewives prefer to cook in glass for they are then able to actually see their foods cooking, eliminating the possibility of improperly cooked foods. Glass is also more easily cleaned than metal utensils, saving time and labor.

A three-fold purpose—bake, serve, and store in the same dish. Fire-King oven glass is not only suitable for oven cooking but makes ideal serving dishes for the table and in addition is safe and practical for refrigerator use.

Not only does Fire-King possess unusual cooking qualities but it is attractive, a complement to any table, and above all—the lowest priced oven glass on the market.

B3405 1 Pt.
B3406 1 Qt.
B3407 1½ Qt.
B3408 2 Qt.

B3445 1 Pt.
B3446 1 Qt.
B3447 1½ Qt.
B3448 2 Qt.

B3466 6⅞ In.
B3467 8⅜ In.
B3469 10⅛ In.

B3497 1½ Qt.
B3498 2 Qt.

Item No.	Size	Doz. to Ctn.	Wt. Ctn.	Retail Price
CASSEROLES WITH KNOB COVERS				
B3405	1 Pint	2	28 lbs.	25c Ea.
B3406	1 Quart	2	51 lbs.	35c Ea.
B3407	1½ Quart	2	63 lbs.	50c Ea.
B3408	2 Quart	1	40 lbs.	60c Ea.
CASSEROLES WITH PIE PLATE COVERS				
B3497	1½ Quart	2	66 lbs.	50c Ea.
B3498	2 Quart	1	37 lbs.	60c Ea.
INDIVIDUAL CASSEROLE & COVER				
B3402	10 Ounce	4	38 lbs.	10c Ea.
OPEN BAKERS				
B3444	1 Pint (Sq.)	4	40 lbs.	15c Ea.
B3445	1 Pint	2	16 lbs.	15c Ea.
B3446	1 Quart	2	29 lbs.	25c Ea.
B3447	1½ Quart	2	35 lbs.	35c Ea.
B3448	2 Quart	1	22 lbs.	40c Ea.
DEEP LOAF PAN				
B3409	9⅛"	2	43 lbs.	35c Ea.
UTILITY PAN				
B3410	10½"	2	45 lbs.	40c Ea.
PIE PLATES				
B3459	8⅜"	4	45 lbs.	10c Ea.
B3460	9"	3	41 lbs.	15c Ea.
B3461	9⅝"	2	35 lbs.	20c Ea.

Item No.	Size	Doz. to Ctn.	Wt. Ctn.	Retail Price
UTILITY BOWLS				
B3466	6⅞"	3	33 lbs.	10c Ea.
B3467	8⅜"	1½	28 lbs.	15c Ea.
B3469	10⅛"	1	25 lbs.	25c Ea.
TRIPLE DUTY JARS AND COVERS				
B3494	4½" x 5"	4	60 lbs.	25c Ea.
B3499	5⅛" x 9⅛"	2	70 lbs.	50c Ea.
INDIVIDUAL DEEP PIE DISH				
B3465	5⅜" x 1⅞"	3	18 lbs.	10c Ea.
INDIVIDUAL BAKERS				
B3413	6 Ounce	6	20 lbs.	5c Ea.
B3420	5 Ounce	6	17 lbs.	5c Ea.
B3421	6 Ounce	6	17 lbs.	5c Ea.

MISCELLANEOUS

Item No.		Doz. to Ctn.	Wt. Ctn.	Retail Price
B3468	8 oz. Nursing Bottle	6	34 lbs.	10c Ea.
B3464	4 oz. Nursing Bottle	6	19 lbs.	10c Ea.
B97	8 oz. Measuring Cup	4	27 lbs.	10c Ea.
B5	2⅛" Percolator Top	6	13 lbs.	5c Ea.
B885	16 oz. Measuring-Mixing Bowl	2	17 lbs.	10c Ea.

B3494 4½ In. x 5 In.
B3499 5⅛ In. x 9⅛ In.

B3420 5 Oz.

B3421 6 Oz.

B3459 8⅜ In.
B3460 9 In.
B3461 9⅝ In.

B3410 10½ In.

B3402 10 Oz.

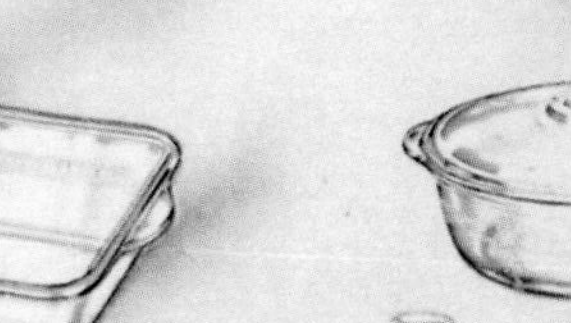

B5 2⅛ In.

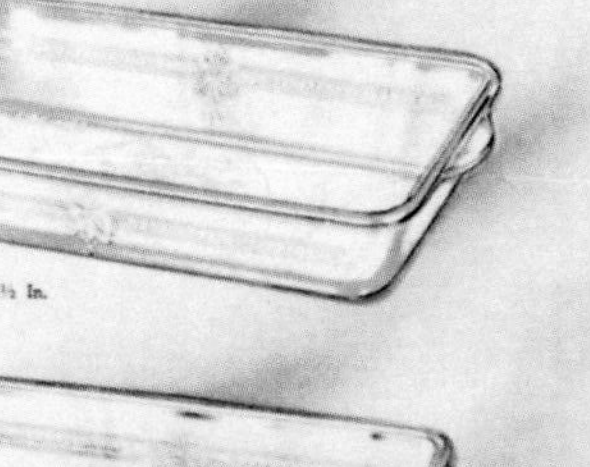

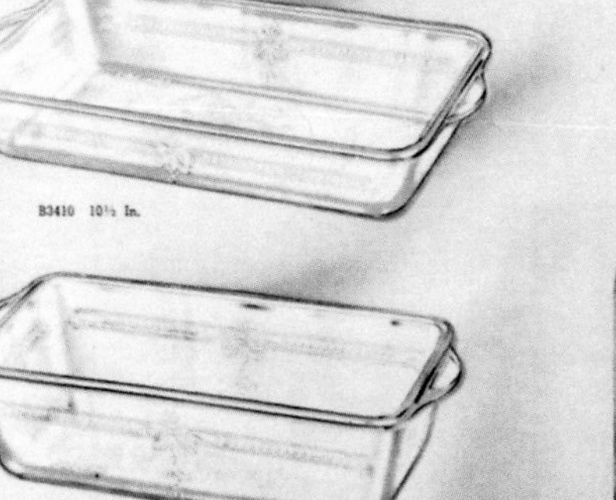

B3465 5⅜ In. x 1⅞ In.

Fry Glass Company, 1901 – 1933

Although Fry produced some plain crystal ovenware beginning around 1917, the Fry ovenware most recognized by collectors is the 1922 patented, heat proof, opalescent-looking Pearl Oven Ware. Pearl's effect was somehow chemically achieved in the heating process when its alumina particle makeup was suspended. It was advertised as being fit to go from oven heat to table service. Though coveted by collectors today, it was not a rousing success at the time and did suffer from some temperature change breakage on occasion. Fry started out making cut glass, but switched to everyday consumer products about the start of WWI. Today, it is more generally recognized by collectors for its kitchen and ovenware items than for its regular lines of tableware products, which are quite remarkable.

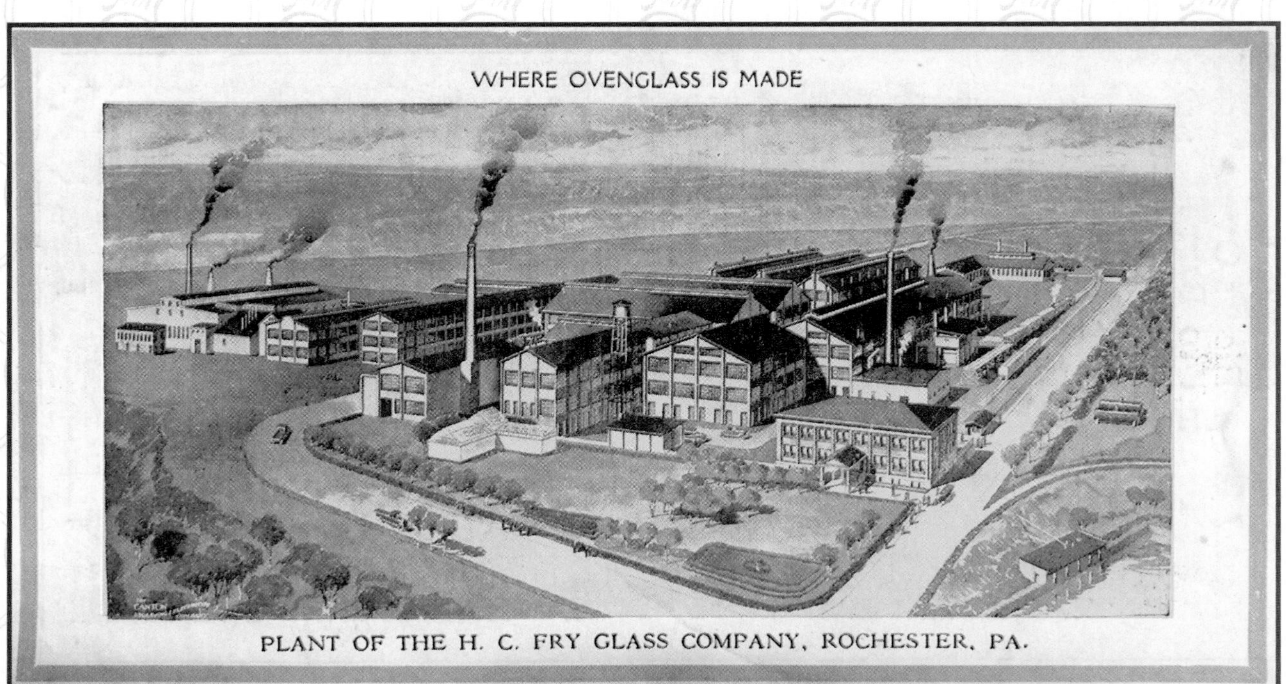

Fry Ovenglass

THIS booklet illustrates glass baking dishes now in general use that are made by the H. C. Fry Glass Co. Fry quality Ovenglass answers all requirements and is giving entire satisfaction. The product is the result of two years of experiments and trials resulting in a glass of high thermal endurance, combining great strength and low expansion. It is pressed into convenient shapes for all kinds of bake-oven dishes. The full resistant power of the glass is scientifically developed by thorough annealing. Expansion and contraction are reduced to a minimum. In baking, the oven heat is transmitted to the food uniformly from all sides, top and bottom, the heat radiating through the glass.

Ovenglass is clean and clear and most appropriate for serving on the dining table, because of its neat appearance and transparency, and its prettily browned provender clearly visible.

The H. C. Fry Glass Co. could not afford to put this Ovenglass on the market untried on account of their international reputation long established as makers of high quality glassware of all kinds; therefore, Fry Quality Ovenglass now measures up to the Fry standard.

How To Use Fry Ovenglass

FRY Ovenglass has twice the strength and more than twice the thermal endurance of other glass; but it is nevertheless glass and must be handled like glass. It does not chip as all edges are round, but it will not withstand knocks as if it were tin or iron. It may break by dropping on the floor or by a sudden blow.

One cannot treat this remarkable glass too carelessly. Ordinary care must be given and it can then be used continuously for years with most satisfactory results, leaving the glass as perfect, clean and handsome as when new.

When removing this glass from the oven use a dry cloth. Ovenglass is made to stand sudden changes from hot to cold or vice-versa but reasonable care should be exercised.

Guarantee

This glass is made for oven use only, and is guaranteed not to break while in the oven if above precautions are heeded.

H. C. FRY GLASS COMPANY

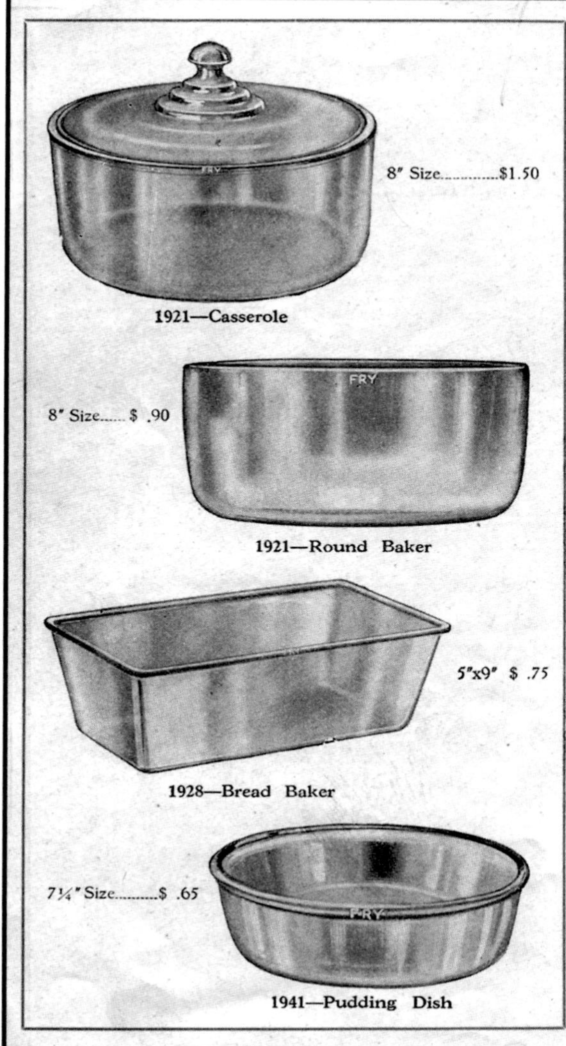

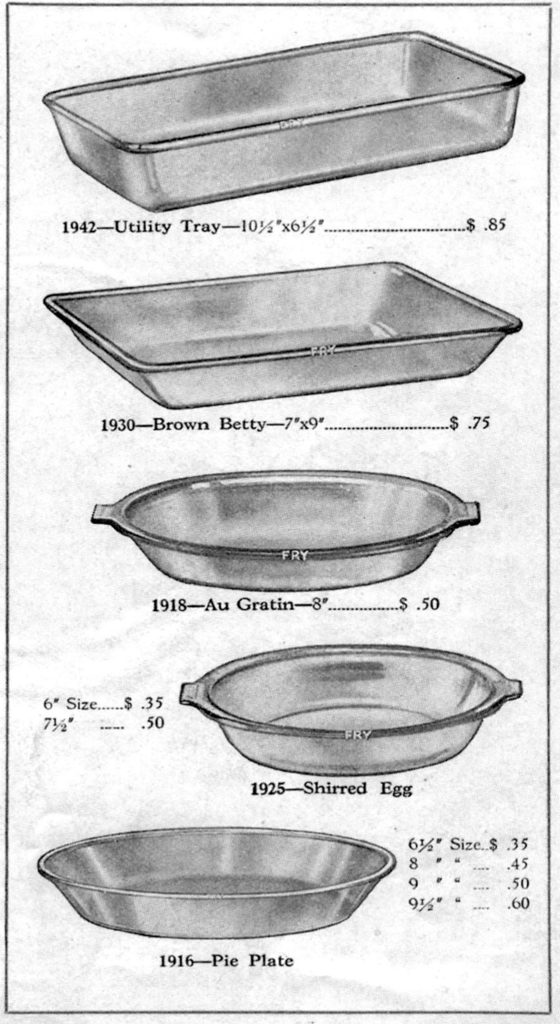

1924—Bean Pot
1½ Pt. ....$ .65

1924—Petite Marmite
1 Pt ....$ .50
12X 1.20

1922—Beef Steak Pie
5" Size........................$ .50

1938—Individual Casserole
4½" Size......................$ 50

1939—Cake Plate
9" Size...........................$ .50

1917—Oval Baker
6" Size ....$ .25
7" " .... .35
8" " .... .50

1931—Mushroom and Cover.......................$ .75

1923—Ramekin
2½ Oz. ....$1.50 Doz.
3 Oz. .... 1.50 Doz.
4 Oz. .... 2.00 Doz.

1940—Cocotte
4½" Size ....$ .20
5¼" " .... .25

1919—Round Baker
6" Size ....$.35

1927—Custard
4 Oz. ....$1.70 Doz.
6 " .... 1.80 Doz.

1937—Baked Apple
4¾"x2¾" Size....................$ .35

1936—Custard
4½ Oz. ....$1.75 Doz.
6 " .... 2.00 Doz.

1926—Cocotte
4½" Size.........................$ .20
5" " .... .25

1929—Percolator Top
2⅞" Size ....$1.50 Doz.

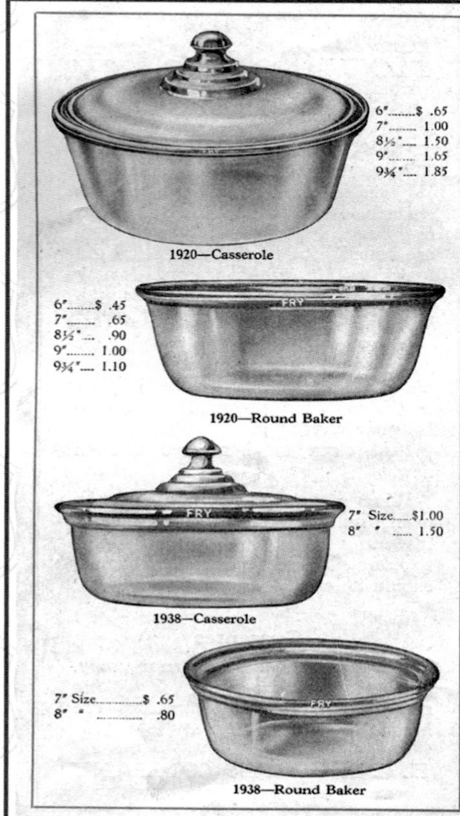

1920—Casserole
6"........$ .65
7"........ 1.00
8½"...... 1.50
9"........ 1.65
9¾"...... 1.85

1920—Round Baker
6"........$ .45
7"........ .65
8½"...... .90
9"........ 1.00
9¾"...... 1.10

1938—Casserole
7" Size......$1.00
8" " 1.50

1938—Round Baker
7" Size..............$ .65
8" " .... .80

1922—Casserole
5" Size......$ .50
7" " 1.10
8" " 1.50
9" " 1.75

1922—Round Baker
7" Size......$ .75
8" " ...... .90
9" " 1.10

1932—Oval Casserole
7" Size......$1.00
8" " 1.20
9" " 1.65

1932—Oval Baker
7" Size.............$ .65
8" " .... .80
9" " 1.00

Oven Glass Assortment No. 2

Packed carefully in cartons ready for shipment. Each box contains the following items:

1—1938—8″ CASSEROLE AND COVER
2—1928—5x9″ BREAD BAKERS
2—1916—9″ PIE PLATES
1—1930—7x9″ BROWN BETTY
1—1924—1½ Pt. BEAN POT
2—1919—6″ ROUND BAKERS
2—1917—6″ OVAL BAKERS
1—1918—8″ OVAL AU GRATIN
6—1923—3 oz. RAMEKIN
6—1936—4½ oz. CUSTARD

24 Pieces

SET COMPLETE INCLUDING CARTON $9.40

Oven Glass Assortment No. 1

Packed carefully in cartons ready for shipment. Each box contains the following items:

1—1938—8″ CASSEROLE AND COVER
1—1928—5x9″ BREAD BAKER
1—1930—7x9″ BROWN BETTY
1—1916—9″ PIE PLATE
1—1919—6″ ROUND BAKER
1—1917—6″ OVAL BAKER
6—1936—4½ oz. CUSTARD

12 Pieces

SET COMPLETE INCLUDING CARTON $5.50

Paper label reads, "This is a 'ROYALLOY' Steel Frame. Dry thoroughly after using and it will serve you well and long." $235.00

Row 1:
- Casserole, 7" square, in holder, w/lid $95.00
- Baker, 2⅛" x 6⅜", pudding $40.00
- Casserole, 8" oval, engraved, in holder, w/lid, ...$55.00

Row 2:
- Brown Betty, 9" $60.00
- Casserole 7" round, engraved sides, w/lid $65.00
- Trivet, 8" (under casserole) $25.00
- Shirred egg, 7½" round $35.00

Row 3:
- Dish, 9¾", vegetable, 2 part $40.00
- Platter, 11", fish, engraved $45.00
- Pie plate, 8½", engraved, in holder $45.00

Row 4:
- Cake, 9" round $35.00
- Cup and saucer, No. 1969 . . . .$35.00
- Pie plate, 10", in metal holder $45.00

Row 5:

Child's toy set
- Pie plate, 5" $65.00
- Casserole, 4½" round, w/lid $75.00
- Ramekin, 2½" $25.00
- Ramekin, 2½" $25.00
- Bread baker, 5" $65.00

Row 6:
- Platter, 17", fish, engraved $85.00
- Casserole, 7" round, embossed w/grapes, w/lid $65.00

Oven glass, 1927, 4 oz., $12.00
Oven glass, 1925, 6 oz., $12.00

Roaster, 1946-14, 14" x 10" x 7½", domed, $225.00

Row 1:
- Bean pot, 1 qt., in holder, w/lid $135.00
- Cream soup, 5¼", ftd. $65.00
- Casserole, 8" round, in holder, w/lid $50.00

Row 2:
- Casserole, 10", oval, w/green finial $135.00
- Sundae glass, "MACO-MFG-CO, VAPOR-RITE, MAYWOOD-ILL" $55.00
- Platter, 9" x 13", oval $60.00

Row 3:
- Casserole, 6" round $35.00
- Baker, 6" round $30.00
- Cocotte, 5" (for indiv. meat, chicken, oyster pies) . .$25.00
- Cocotte, 4" $25.00
- Custard cup, 4½ oz. $25.00

Row 4:
- Snack plate, 6" x 9", w/cup $50.00
- Mushroom baker/round shirred egg, 6" .$145.00
- Baker, 6", oval $35.00
- Apple baker or custard, 4¾" $32.00

Row 5:
- Butter pat (?), "Fry's Heat Resisting Glass" .$12.00
- Ramekin, 3" $18.00
- Custard cup, 4 or 6 oz. (1927 or 1936) $12.00
- Custard cup, 4 or 6 oz. (1927 or 1936) $12.00
- Custard cup, 6 oz., engraved (1927 or 1936) $14.00
- Custard cup, 6 oz., engraved (1927 or 1936) $14.00
- Custard cup, 4 or 6 oz. (1927 or 1936) $12.00

Row 6:
- Casserole, 7" round, engraved, w/blue finial $135.00
- Ramekin, 2½", "Pearl" or "Lime glass" $25.00
- Ramekin, 2½", "Pearl" or "Lime glass" $25.00
- Server, 8 sided, oval, engraved, 6½" x 9" w/holder $50.00

GLASBAK/GLASBAKE
by McKee, 1917 – 1951

GLASBAKE
by McKee Division of Thatcher Glass Corp., 1951 – 1961

GLASBAKE
by Jeannette, 1961 – 1983

Originally spelled *Glasbak* (as you can see by the catalogs pictured), this ware was also known as *Glasbake* (with an *e*) in subsequent productions. The later (after 1961) Jeannette items usually have a *J* prefix followed by a number on the bottom of each piece.

Note the boxed set of Cameo "with Urn," an appellation addendum used to distinguish this pattern from the Cameo head customarily thought of as Cameo. This box is marked "Glasbake by McKee," but the Currier and Ives boxed set is Glasbake by Jeannette. Currier and Ives is another pattern produced on both Federal and Fire-King wares.

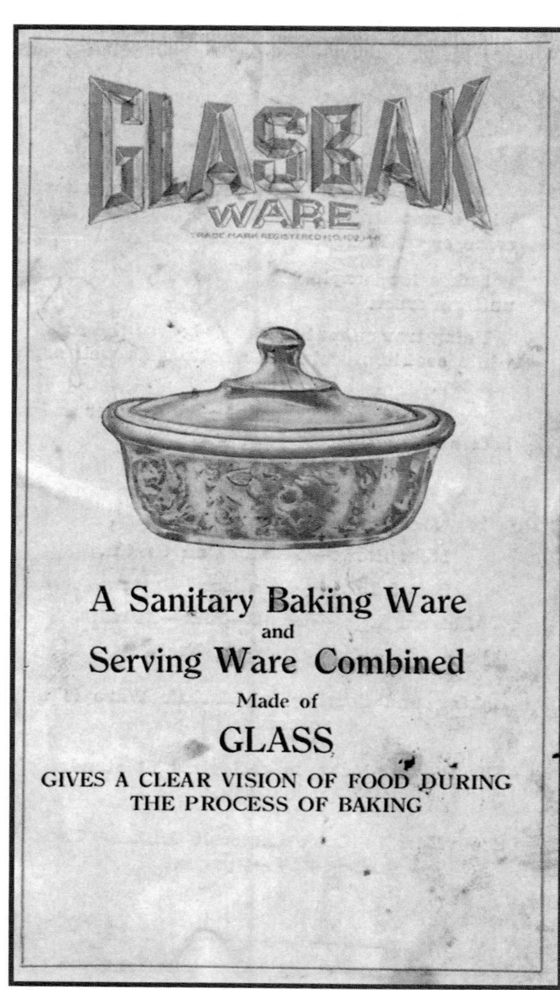

GLASBAK WARE

All inside measurements.

OVAL BAKING OR PUDDING DISHES.
No. 234—8½ in. x 6 in. x 3¼ in.—Capacity 2 Qts.
No. 235—7½ in. x 5⅜ in. x 2¼ in.—Capacity 1 Qt.

ROUND PIE PLATES.
No. 244—9 in.
No. 245—8 in.

ROUND CAKE PLATE.
No. 248—8½ in. x 1 in.

5

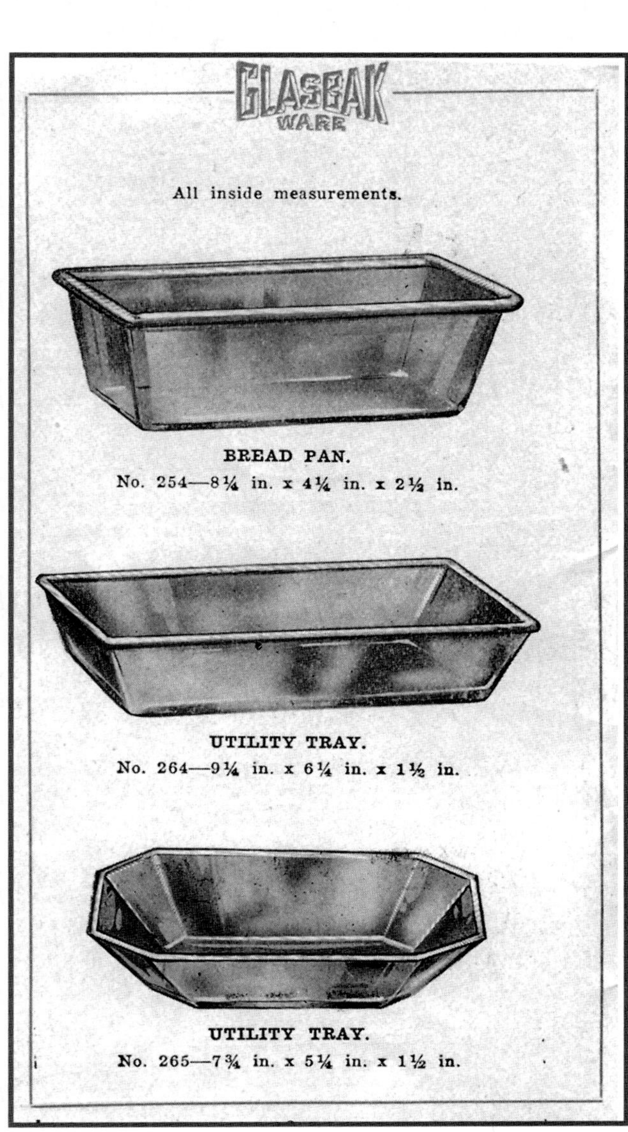
GLASBAK WARE

All inside measurements.

BREAD PAN.
No. 254—8¼ in. x 4¼ in. x 2½ in.

UTILITY TRAY.
No. 264—9¼ in. x 6¼ in. x 1½ in.

UTILITY TRAY.
No. 265—7¾ in. x 5¼ in. x 1½ in.

All inside measurements.

OVAL SHIRRED EGG DISH.
No. 274—7¼ in. x 4½ in. x ⅝ in.

SHIRRED EGG CUP for Mounters.
No. 276—3½ in. x 2 in.—6 Oz.

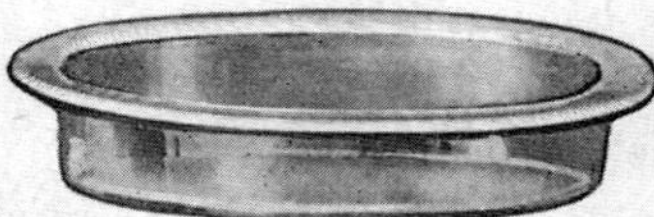

ROUND SHIRRED EGG DISH.
No. 275—4½ in. x 1 in. with ½ in. flange.

ROUND RAMEKINS.
No. 294—2½ in. x 1 in.—3 Oz.
No. 295—3 in. x 1½ in.—4 Oz.

7

All inside measurements.

ROUND CUSTARD CUPS.
No. 284—3½ in. x 1 in.—6 Oz.
No. 285—3⅛ in. x 1¼ in.—4 Oz.

OVAL MUSHROOM and COVER.
No. 304—7¼ in. x 4½ in. x ⅝ in. oval dish **and 4 in.** Bell Cover.

BEAN POT AND COVER.
No. 331—Capacity 1 Pt.

8

All inside measurements.

BOUILLON CUP AND SAUCER.
No. 340—3⅝ in. x 2¼ in. x 1⅛ in.—9 Oz. **Cup and** 6 in. Saucer.

ROUND COCOTTE.
No. 320—Capacity 6 Oz.

PERCOLATOR TOPS.
No. 314—Colonial.
No. 315—Plain.

9

GLASBAKE WARE

ROUND PUDDING DISHES UNCOVERED

No. 190—6⅞x2¾ in. Ea. $0.85
No. 191—5 5/16x2¼ in.... .60
No. 192—4 5/16x2¼ in.... .40

ROUND CASSEROLES AND COVERS

No. 204—2½ Quart Ea. $2.50
No. 205—2 Quart 2.00
No. 206—1½ Quart 1.75
No. 207½—1¼ Quart 1.75
No. 207—1 Quart 1.50
No. 208—1 Pint 1.00
No. 209—½ Pint .... .70

SQUARE CASSEROLES AND COVERS

No. 211—1½ Quart Ea. $1.75
No. 212—1 Quart 1.50

ROUND BAKERS UNCOVERED

No. 214—2½ Quart Ea. $1.40
No. 215 2 Quart 1.20
No. 216—1½ Quart 1.00
No. 217—1 Quart .... .85
No. 218—1 Pint .... .60
No. 219—½ Pint .... .50

SQUARE BAKERS UNCOVERED

No. 221—1½ Quart Ea. $1.00
No. 222—1 Quart .... .85

OVAL CASSEROLES AND COVERS

No. 224—2 Quart ....Ea. $2.00
No. 224½—1½ Qt. 1.75
No. 225—1 Quart 1.50

OVAL BAKERS UNCOVERED

No. 234—2 Quart ....Ea. $1.20
No. 234½—1½ Qt. 1.00
No. 235—1 Quart .... .85

ROUND SHALLOW CASSEROLE AND COVER

No. 507—1 Qt. .... Ea. 1.50
No. 541—9½ in. ..
Raised Cover Ea. $1.90

OVAL SHALLOW BAKERS HANDLED Each

No. 239—10½x8½x2¾" $1.25
No. 240—9¾x7¾x1⅞" 1.00
No. 241—8½x6½x1⅝" .85

ROUND PIE PLATES

No. 242—11¾x1½ in. Ea. $1.10
No. 243—10½x1½ in. 1.00
No. 244—9⅝x1½ in. .... .90
No. 244½—9x1⅜ in. ...... .75
No. 245—8¾x1⅜ in. .... .75
No. 246—8 x1⅜ in. .... .60
No. 247—6½x1⅜ in. ...... .50
No. 247½—4⅞x1⅛ in. .. .25

SAVE ALL PIE PLATE

No. 1—10⅝x1½ in. Ea. $1.10
No. 2—9½x1½ in. 1.00
No. 3—9 x1¼ in. .... .90

ROUND CAKE PLATE

No. 248—9⅛x1¼ in. Ea. $0.75

SQUARE CAKE PANS

No. 250—9x1¼ in. ..Ea. $1.00
No. 251—5x1 in. .... .50

INDIVIDUAL OVAL BAKERS

No. 236—6¼ in. ......Ea. $0.40
No. 237—5⅛ in. .... .30

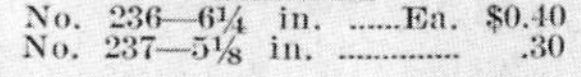

OBLONG BREAD PANS Each

No. 253—10½x5½x3⅛" $1.50
No. 254—9⅛x5⅛x2⅞" .. .90
No. 254½—8x4x2½" ...... .75
No. 255—9¼x3¼x3" .... .75
No. 253—4¼x3x1¾" .... .25

OBLONG UTILITY TRAYS Each

No. 263—12⅝x8⅛x2 in. $1.75
No. 264—10½x6½x2 in. 1.00
No. 265—8¾x6 x2 in. .85

AU-GRATIN DISH HANDLED

No. 274—5⅞x1½ in. Ea. $0.65

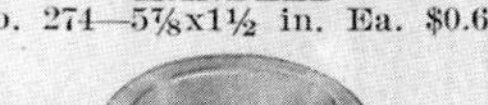

ROUND SHIRRED EGG DISH

No. 275—5⅞x1½ in. Ea. $0.50

FRENCH CUSTARD CUP

No. 283—4 oz. .... Ea. $0.20

ROUND CUSTARD CUPS

No 284—6 oz. .... Ea. $0.25
No. 285—4 oz. .... .20
No. 286—3 oz. .... .10

GLASBAK WARE

MOUNTED GLASBAKE WARE
Guaranteed Glasbake Ware With
Nickel Plated Servers

ROUND COVERED CASSEROLES
No. 206—1½ Qt. Ea. $2.60
No. 207—1 Qt. 2.40

SQUARE COVERED CASSEROLES
No. 211—1½ Qt. Ea. $3.20
No. 212—1 Qt. 3.00

ROUND PIE PLATE
No. 244½—9 in. Ea. $1.50

OBLONG UTILITY DISH
No 263—12⅝" ....Ea. $3.00
No. 264—10½" 2.40
No. 265—8⅝" 2.10

OVAL COVERED CASSEROLES
No. 224—2 Qt. ....Ea. $3.30
No. 225—1 Qt. 2.60

OVAL SHALLOW BEEFSTEAK CASSEROLES —COVERED
No. 549—1½ Qt. Ea. $3.20

No. 378—15⅝x10¾x1⅝ **Well and Tree Platter**
Steel N. P. Frame Ea. 4.60 P.&B. Brass Frame Ea. 5.85

GLASBAK WARE

No. 1 HOUSEHOLD SET

Price, each $6.35

Consists of
1— 1½ Qt. Casserole and Cover
1— 9⅛" Bread Pan
2— 9⅜" Pie Plates
1—10½" Utility Tray
6—4 Oz. Custards

No. 4 HOUSEHOLD SET

Price, each $4.40

Consists of
1— 1½ Qt. Casserole and Cover
1— 9⅛" Bread Pan
1— 9⅜" Pie Plate
1—10½" Utility Tray

No. 5 GIFT SET

Price, each $5.25

Consists of
1—1½ Qt. Oval Beefsteak Casserole and Cover
1—9⅛" Bread Pan
1—9⅜" Pie Plate
1—9" Square Cake Pan
1—8¾" Utility Tray

GLASBAKE WARE

BOULLION CUP AND SAUCER

No. 340—9 oz. .... Ea. $0.85
No. 340—Cup only .... .45
No. 340—Saucer only .... .40

DEEP OVAL PLATTER

No. 369—15⅝ in. $2.00

OVAL FISH PLATTERS

No. 370—15 in. .... Ea. $2.00
No. 371—13 in. 1.50

OVAL MEAT PLATTER

No. 375—13x9x1⅝" Ea. $1.20

WELL AND TREE PLATTER

No. 378—15⅝ in. .... Ea. $3.00

OBLONG BISCUIT TRAY

Each
No. 266—9⅛x7⅝x1¼" $0.85

PARTITION VEGETABLE DISHES

Each
No. 345—10½x8½x2⅜" $1.75
No. 346—9¾x7¾x1⅞" 1.50

TUBE CAKE PAN

No. 352—9x3½ in. Ea. $2.00

MUFFIN PANS

Each
No. 361—8 Compartment 1.60
No. 362—6 Compartment 1.35

RAMEKINS OR COCOTTES

No. 294—3 oz. Per Doz. $1.80
No. 295—4 oz. Per Doz. 2.40
No. 320—6 oz. Per Doz. 3.00

MUSHROOM DISH AND COVER

No. 303—6x4½ in. Ea. $1.15
No. 303—Bell Covers Ea. .50

BAKED APPLE DISHES

No. 310—5½x3 in. Ea. $0.75
No. 311—4¾x2¾ in. .... .50

GRILL **SERVICE PLATES** **SOUP**

No. 390—Grill 10½ in. .... Ea. $1.25
No. 391—Service 10½ in. 1.00
No. 392—Soup 8½ in. 1.00
No. 393—Grill 9 in. 1.00

COVERED MEAT LOAF DISHES

Each
No. 381—9⅛x5⅛x2⅞" $1.75

OVAL SHALLOW BAKING DISH WITH TWO HANDLED COVER

No. 410—10x7⅝x2⅞" Ea $2.00

COOKING CUP

Each
No. 420—8 oz. 3⅛x3¼x2½" .50

HOT DISH TRAY

No. 400—8x8x1 in. ..Ea. $0.75

SHALLOW BEEF STEAK COVERED

No. 549—10⅝x7¼x2⅞" Ea 1.75

ROUND PARTITION VEGETABLE DISH

No. 355—11⅜x1½" Ea. $1.80

STANDARD PERCOLATOR TOPS

No. 314—Colonial ..Ea. $0.10
No. 315—Plain .... .10

COVERED BEAN POTS

No. 328—2 Quart ....Ea. $2.50
No. 329—1½ Quart 2.25
No. 330—1 Quart 1.75
No. 331—1 Pint 1.00

Casserole, 9½" w, rolled handle	$12.00
Lid	$10.00
Bowl, 8¼"	$10.00
Casserole, 8⅜" with handles, w/7¾" round lid	$15.00

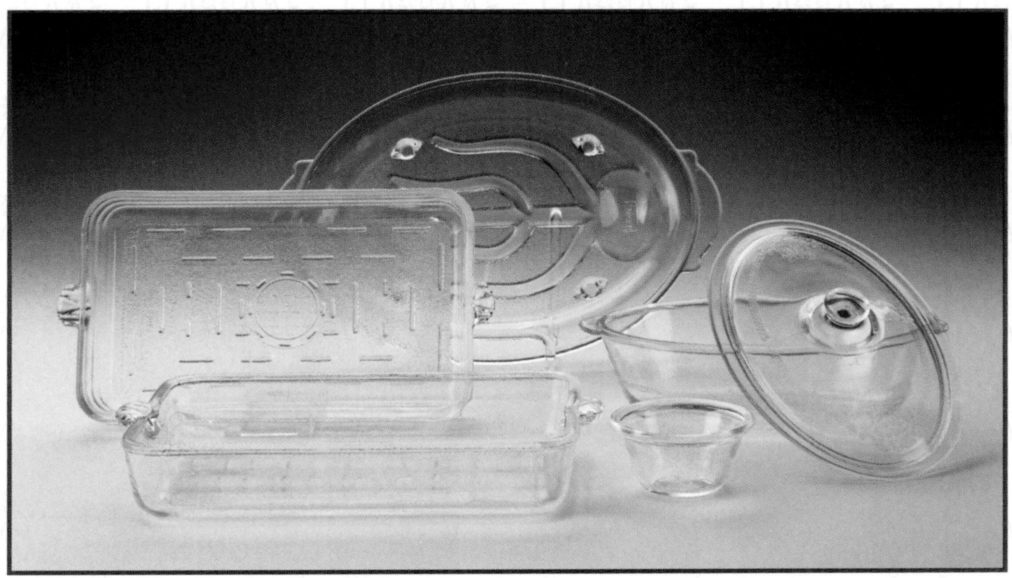

Platter, Well & Tree	$15.00
Tray, utility, oblong	$12.00
Loaf pan, Mary Dunbar	$25.00
Casserole, oval, with lid	$15.00
Custard	$3.00

Colors – *Crystal*

Tray, 8⅝"..$12.00
Custard, 3 9/16" $3.00
Baker, 2 15/16" x 4 7/16", rectangular..$8.00
Baker, 6 5/16" x 4 3/16", oval...$10.00
Custard, 3⅜" $3.00

Loaf pan, 5" x 9", $12.00
Casserole, J514, 2 qt., with lid, $15.00

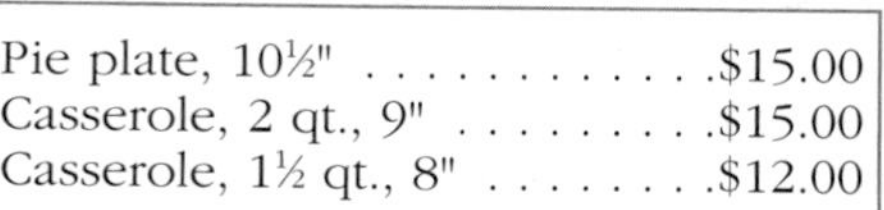

Pie plate, 10½" $15.00
Casserole, 2 qt., 9" $15.00
Casserole, 1½ qt., 8" $12.00

Oven/refrigerator, 4" x 5"	$12.00 each
Cake pan, angel food	$15.00

Queen Anne

Baker, ring mold	$9.50
Baker, handled	$5.00
Casserole, handled, w/cover	$15.00

Glass Cookware

Beautiful, practical, efficient

Guaranteed I year against heat breakage

NEW MODERN DESIGN OVENWARE FLAMEX

- Smart enough to serve at your festive table. Each piece has gleaming tropical flower design
- Use same dish for . . . cooking . . . serving . . . storing
- Look while you cook without lifting a cover
- Each dish leads a double life with 2 or more uses
- Light in weight yet strong with easy-grip handles
- Non-porous finish is sanitary, never absorbs odors
- Easy to clean. Always looks sparkling, bright

10-piece homemaker's Flamex set

$1.49 Complete

Prove to yourself how efficient Flamex ovenware is with this starter set that does so many baking jobs. Sears smart, practical Flamex ovenware costs so little. And you save when you buy the set.

Consists of: 1½-qt. **covered casserole.** Use bottom as open baking dish, top as a cake pan; 8-inch diameter, 1¼-in. high. **One 12⅝x8½x2½-in. utility baking dish. One 9½x1¼-in. pie plate** and **6 custard cups,** each, 4 ounce size. Shipping weight, of set, 7 pounds 8 ounces.

11 D 04944—10-piece set **$1.49**

Now! Oven Roaster of Flamex Glass

$2.25

Oven Roaster 12⅝x8½x6½ inches

Enjoy the thrill of baking a delicious, tender roast, chicken or ham in Flamex . . . heat-resisting glass ovenware. No more burned fingers because without lifting the cover you can see food browning evenly, on all sides. Flamex absorbs heat quickly, holds it. Special self-locking cover stays in place. Use bottom as 12⅝x8½x4-in. loaf pan; cover 12⅝x8½x2½-in. baking dish.

11 D 4929—12⅝x8½x6½ in high. Wt., 7 lbs . . . $2.25

Baking and Refrigerator set

95c

Just see what this **6-piece** utility set does. Has so many uses: 1. Bake meat, beans, vegetables. 2. Serve them at the table using covers as trays. 3. Store leftover food in refrigerator by setting one on the other. 4. They take very little space on the pantry shelf because they nest so compactly.

Set includes: 10-oz. dish, diam. 4 in.; 1¼-pt. dish, diam. 5 in.; and 2½-qt. dish, diam. 6 in. All with covers.

11 D 04942—Shpg. wt., 5 lbs. **95c**

Open Casserole

28c 1 Qt.

A good starter piece for your Flamex set. Better still, buy two of one size for an efficient small roaster . . . they lock together tightly.

11 D 4926—State size wanted.

1-qt., 7-in. diam. Wt., 1 lb. **28c**
1½-qt., 8-in. diam. Wt., 1 lb. 8 oz. . . . **37c**
2-qt., 9-in. diam. Wt., 2 lbs. **46c**
3-qt., 10-in. diam. Wt., 3 lbs. **57c**

11 D 4925—Utility Baking Dish . . . *Cake Pan.* Shown as cover for above casserole.
7-in. diam. 1¼ in. high. Wt., 1 lb. **14c**
8-in. diam. 1¼ in. high. Wt., 1 lb. 4 oz. . **19c**
9-in. diam. 1¼ in. high. Wt., 1 lb. 8 oz. . . **22c**
10-in. diam. 1¼ in. high. Wt., 1 lb. 12 oz. **28c**

Covered Casserole

42c 1 Qt.

See its many uses: open baking dish, covered casserole, covered baker. Use cover separately for cake pan. Pieces fit together tightly.

11 D 4924 State size.

1-qt. Shpg. wt., 2 lbs. 8 oz. **42c**
1½-qt. Shpg. wt., 3 lbs. **56c**
2-qt. Shpg. wt., 3 lbs. 4 oz. **65c**
3-qt. Shpg. wt., 4 lbs. 12 oz. **85c**

Covered Loaf Dish

79c

No half-done foods when you bake in Flamex. You can see food brown on all sides—on the bottom. Meat loaf, small roast can be whisked to the table in this sparkling glass modern design loaf dish. Keeps food piping hot for late-comers. Top is self-locking. Use bottom as loaf pan, top as utility baking dish. Cover, 10¼x5x1½ in., bottom, 10¼x5x2¾ in.; overall size: 10¼x5x4¾ in.

11 D 4934—Covered Loaf Dish. Shpg. wt., 3 lbs. **79c**

Pie Plates

22c 9½x1¼ in.

Count on flaky, crunchy crusts every time. Bottom crusts brown beautifully . . . glass absorbs heat. Serve your prize pie right from the same dish . . . the way smart hostesses do. Wide rim keeps juices in . . . easy to slip pie out. Convenient side handles.

11 D 4928—State size wanted.

9½x1¼ in. high. Wt., 1 lb. 8 oz. . **22c**
10½x1¼ in. high. Wt., 2 lbs. **27c**

Custard Cups

27c For 6

Set the pace in your crowd—serve each person an individual portion in a distinctive glass dish . . . gelatine dessert, salad, pudding or ice cream. Or use these heat-resistant glass custard cups to brown custards, popovers, to a turn. Heat and serve baby's vegetable in them. 4-ounce size. Included in Flamex set above. Shipping weight for 6, 1 pound 12 ounces.

11 D 4937—Custard cups. . . . 6 for **27c**

Loaf Pans

37c 10¼x5x2¾ in.

Make delicious cake or bread. Bake meat loaf or fish and bring it directly to the table. Glass keeps food hot for the tardy ones in your family. Convenient side handles. You'll find Flamex easy to clean . . . without endless scouring.

11 D 4927—10¼x5x2¾ in. high. Shipping weight, 1 lb. 8 oz. **37c**

11 D 4933—12⅝x8½x4 in. high. Shipping weight, 4 lbs. **$1.70**

Utility Dishes

42c 10¼x5x1½ in.

Popular baking dish—for apples, meats or fish, etc. A sparkling glass deep platter or serving tray for salads . . . the dish with a hundred uses.

11 D 4936—State size wanted.

10¼x5x1½ in. Wt., 1 lb. 8 oz. . . . **42c**
12⅝x8½x2½ in. Wt., 3 lbs. **55c**

PAGE 731 . . . HOUSEWARES

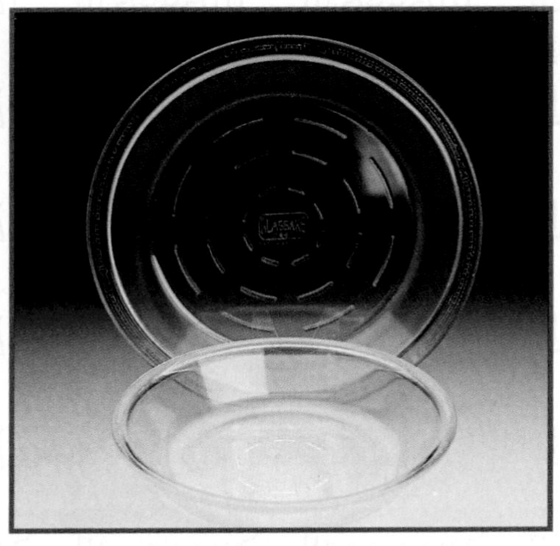

Pie plate, 9¼", Sealtest, $7.50
Pie plate, 6¾", Sealtest, $8.00

Glasbake, #55, 8⅞" wide
(including handle, 10"), $30.00

Casserole lid	$20.00
Casserole bottom	$15.00
Baker	$20.00

Heart items generally attributed to Glasbake, but label says "Saben Glass Co."

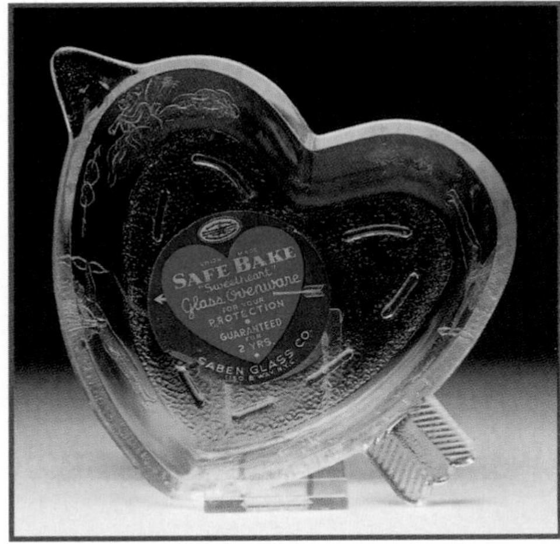

Safe Bake Heart, with label, $25.00

Patterns – *"Blue Floral"*

10¼", 2½ qt.	$18.00
8", 1½ qt.	$15.00
6½", 1½ pt.	$12.00

Casserole, J2352, 2 qt., 2 part	$15.00
Casserole, J514, 2 qt.	$10.00
Loaf pan, J522	$12.00

Patterns – *"Blue Fruit"*

Casserole, J235, 1 qt., 6⅛" x 9⅞", with lid, $15.00
Casserole, 1½ pt., 7¼" x 2$^{15}/_{16}$", $10.00

Patterns – *"Brown Floral"*

Casserole, J235, 1 qt., with lid, $12.50

Patterns – *Cameo*

Casserole, 2 qt., with lid, $25.00
Square baker, J247, 9", $22.00

Casserole, J512, 1½ qt., round	$22.00
Casserole, J2057, 5" round, French handled	$15.00
Lid, J313	$4.00

Patterns – *Cameo "with Urn"*

Casserole, J514, 2 qt., with lid, $27.50
Utility dish, J263, 2½ qt., 13⅞" x 8⅛", $25.00

Patterns – *Cameo "with Urn"*

Item	Price
Casserole, 1 qt.	$20.00
Casserole, 1½ qt.	$22.00
Casserole, 2 qt.	$25.00
Baker, rectangular	$25.00
Baker, square	$22.00
Set in box	$135.00

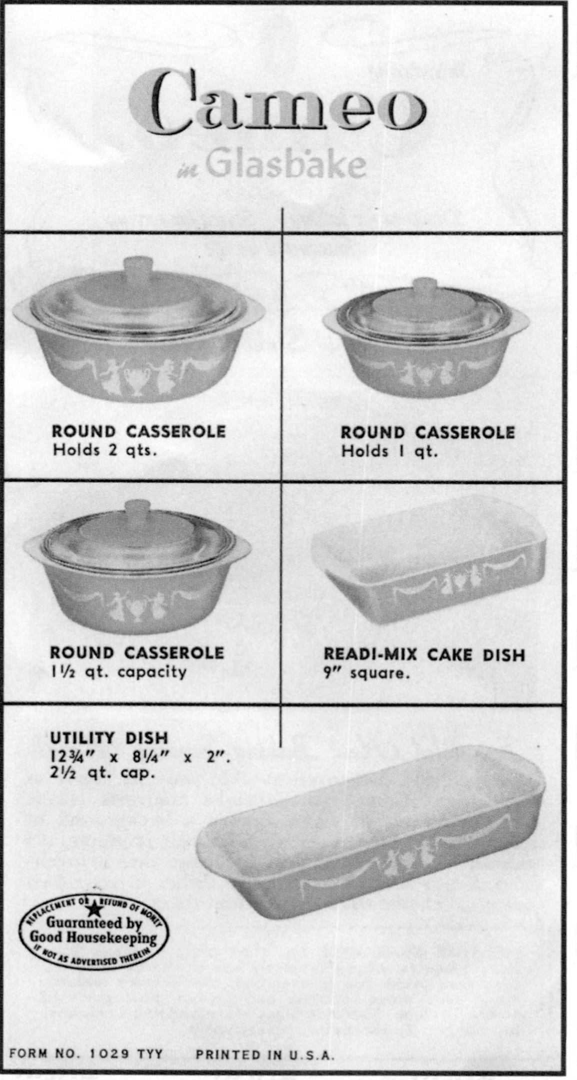

Custard, J2018, 4", $8.00
French casserole, J2632, 14 oz., 5", $12.50

Casserole, J2352, 2 qt., $20.00
Loaf pan, J522, 1½ qt., $22.00

Jeannette 12-piece ovenware set, $165.00

Glasbake

Patterns – *Daisy Days*

Casserole, J225, 6¼" x 10", 1 qt., $15.00
French Casserole, $10.00

Patterns – *"Fleur de Lis"*

Casserole, J235, 1 qt., $15.00

Patterns – *"Grecian"*

Rectangular baker, 2½ qt., $15.00

Patterns – *"Green Floral"*

Bowl, J2352, $12.00
Square baker, J2428, $12.00

Bowl, J514, 2 qt., $10.00
Casserole, J2352, 2 part, $12.00

Patterns – *"Ivy"*

Item	Price
Tumbler, 5 oz.	$6.00
Tumbler, 9 oz.	$8.00
Loaf pan, J522, 1½ qt.	$12.50

Rectangular baker, J263, 2½ qt., $18.00

Patterns – *Mushroom*

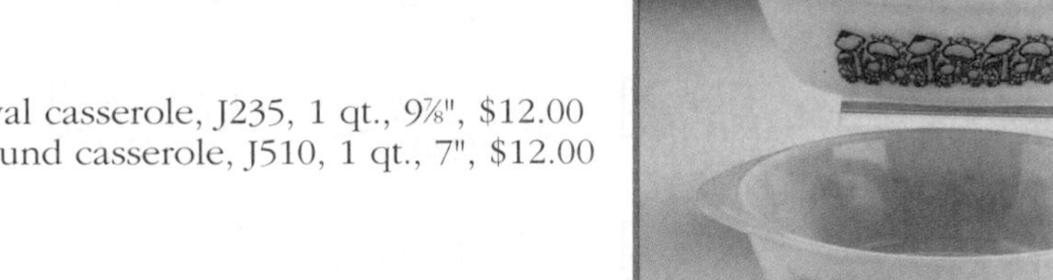

Oval casserole, J235, 1 qt., 9⅞", $12.00
Round casserole, J510, 1 qt., 7", $12.00

Patterns – *"Red Floral"*

Baker, 12", divided	$20.00
Cereal bowl, 5"	$12.00
Custard, 4"	$8.00
Loaf pan, 1½ qt.	$15.00
Mug	$12.50

Patterns – *"Snowflake"*

Rectangular casserole, 1½ qt., J805, $15.00
Rectangular baker, J263, 2½ qt., divided, $15.00

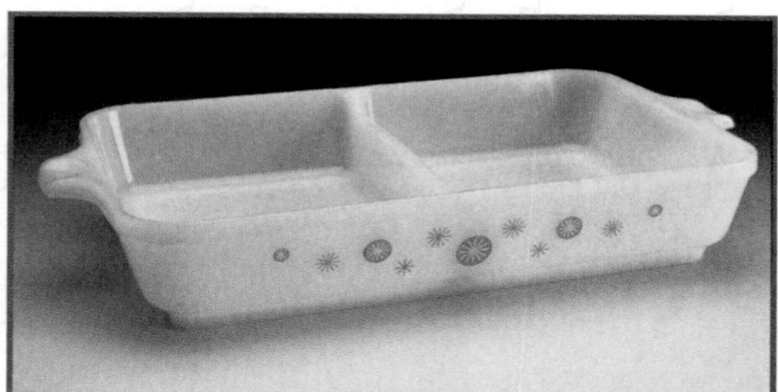

Snowflake-type rectangular baker, J2335, 2½ qt., 14 7/16" x 8", divided, $18.00

Patterns – *Wheat*

Mug, $10.00
Bowl, 12 oz., 5", marked "Sears," $12.50

Butter dish, 6", $60.00
Refrigerator dish, 5" x 4⅛", $28.00
Refrigerator dish, 5" x 9", $35.00

Canisters: 48 oz., $65.00; 40 oz., $60.00; 24 oz., $40.00

Items – *Bakers & Casseroles*

Rectangular baker/refrigerator, J257, 1 qt., 8", $10.00
Baker/refrigerator, J258, 1 pt., 5⅛", $8.00

Loaf pans, J522, 1½ qt.,
$10.00 – 12.00 each

Loaf pan, J522, 1½ qt., non-stick interior, pebble bottom, $15.00

Baker, J257, 8" x 5", w/cover, $18.00

Baker, J235, oval, $8.00
Divided baker, J2352, oval, $12.00

Casserole, 2½ qt., $15.00

GUARANTEE

Glasbake ware is made for oven use only. It is guaranteed not to break while in the oven and if such breakage should occur the item broken will be replaced free of charge if below precautions are heeded.

HOW TO USE GLASBAKE WARE

1. Do not take it out of the oven with a wet cloth.
2. Do not knock it against glass or when hot let it come in contact too suddenly with water or cold metal.
3. Do not put it directly over a blaze.

On Glasbake Ware is featured the "Heat-Quick" Bottom. The small corrugations on the base of the vessel allow the complete radiation of the heat, which gives the food an even baking all through with a uniform crust.

The "HEAT-QUICK" bottom enables the housewife to bake more quickly, evenly and to save oven fuel.

Casseroles, J235, 1 qt.	
Blue, with lid	$16.00
White, with lid	$14.00
Blue design, with lid	$18.00
Lid only	$8.00

Casserole, J2274, 1 qt., $15.00

Casserole, J235, 1 qt., 10" w/handle, "1982 Watkins," $12.00

Bowl, J2427, 1½ qt., $12.00

Oval baker, 1½ pt., 7¾", $8.00
Oval baker, 2½ qt., 12¾", $15.00

Oval baker, $6.00
Oval baker, J314, 2 qt., $12.00

Hen baker, J2482, 7½" wide, $30.00

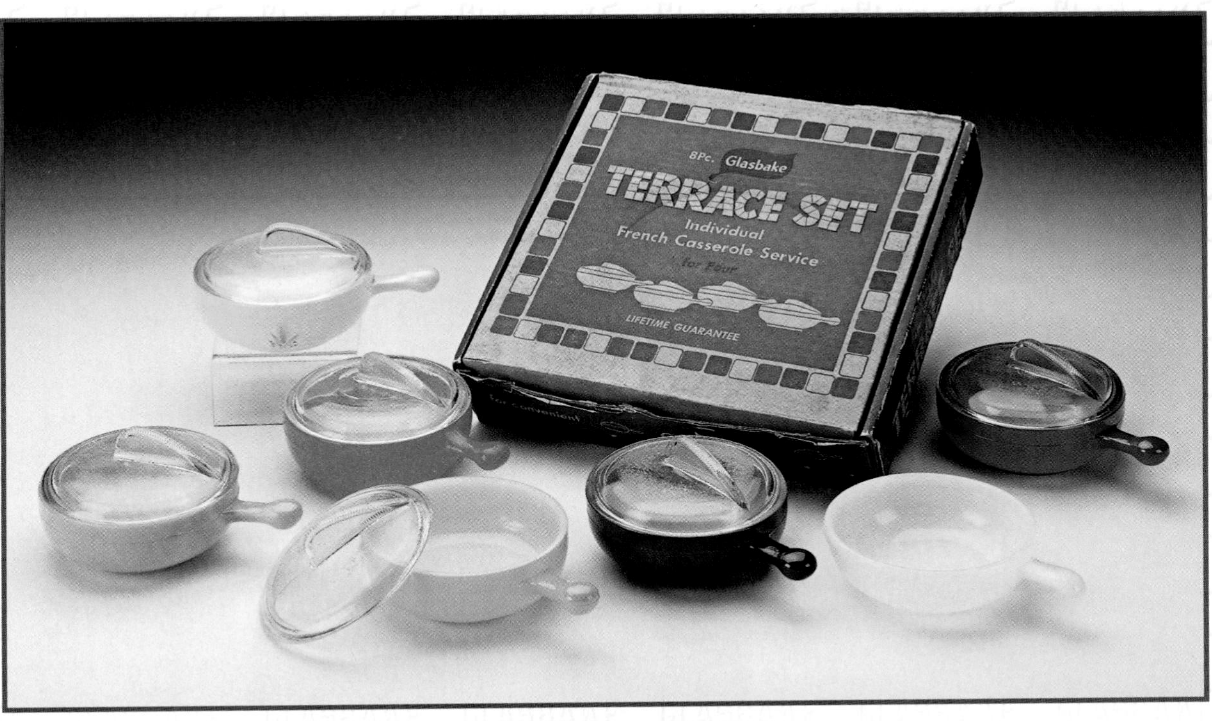

Casseroles, individual	
Dark colors	$12.00 each
Regular colors	$9.00 each
Four dark colors in box	$65.00
Lids	$4.00 each

Individual casserole, J2057-24, 5", with Prairie View ad on lid, $25.00

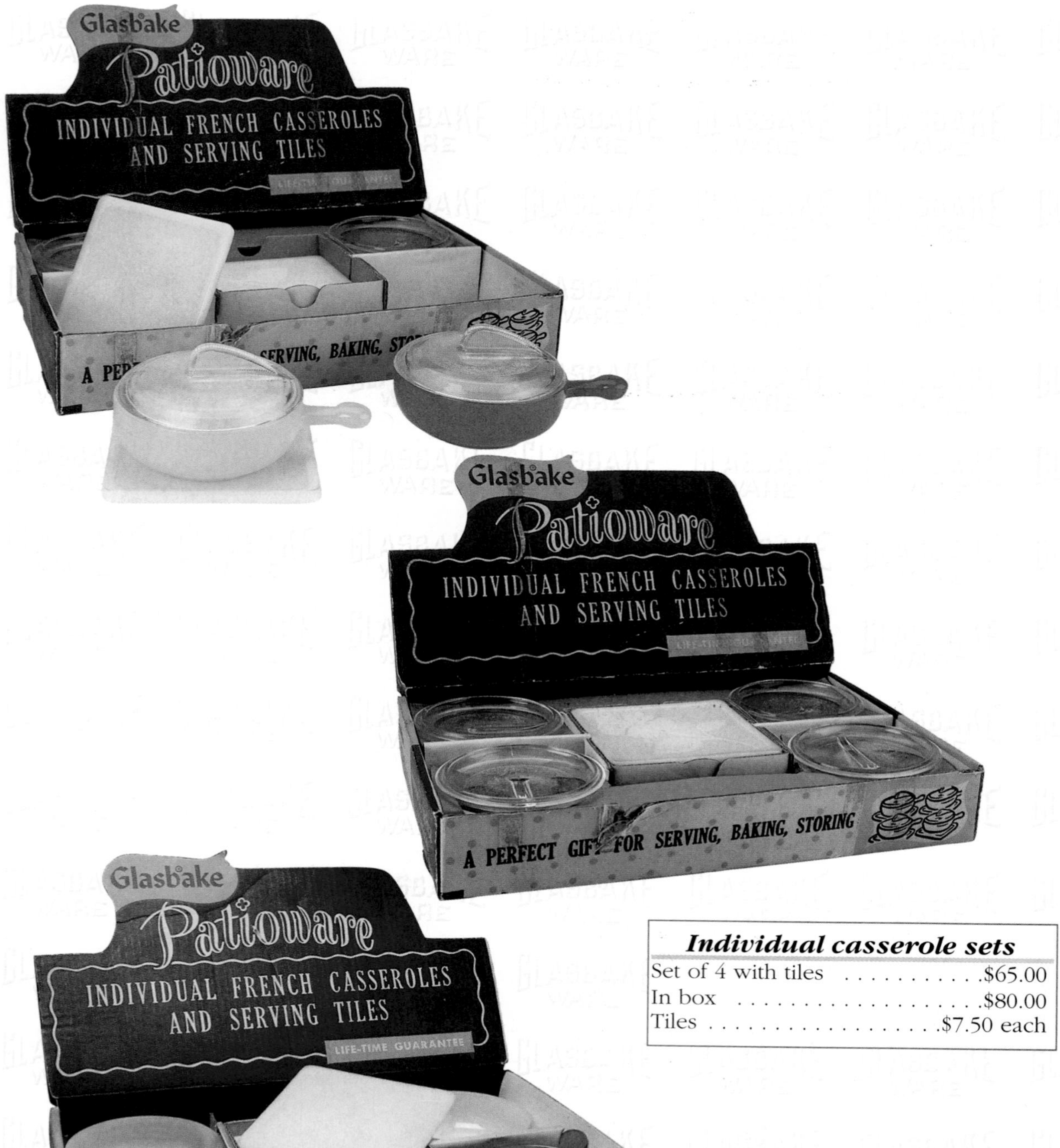

Individual casserole sets	
Set of 4 with tiles	$65.00
In box	$80.00
Tiles	$7.50 each

RECIPE FOR DEVILED CRABS

APPROXIMATE SERVING: SIX

1 teaspoon dry mustard
1 teaspoon salt
¼ teaspoon pepper
1 cup milk
2 hard boiled eggs, minced

1 lb. crabmeat
4 tablespoons butter
3 tablespoons flour
1 tablespoon minced parsley
2 teaspoons lemon juice

½ cup bread or cracker crumbs

Melt butter in sauce pan, add flour, stir until smooth; add parsley, mustard, lemon juice, salt, pepper, milk and stir until smooth. Add crabmeat and eggs, and stir until well mixed. Remove from heat, and when cool enough to handle, place mixture in six Crabshell Baking Dishes. Sprinkle with Bread crumbs, and bake in hot oven until brown on top, or if preferred they may be broiled under very low flame. If you wish them to be extra rich in flavor, dot each crab with butter.

If one prefers a dry Crab, eliminate the flour and milk, and mix other ingredients cold (no cooking) using considerable more butter (melted) and mixing about two cups soft white bread. About half teaspoon onion juice adds bit of spice.

Our recipe is described as simply as possible and we have had many favorable comments upon it. We suggest, that you try a variant of spices which you may be fond to season your Crabmeat, and in making your deviled Crabs, may strike some particular combination that is very pleasing.

Always remember that the larger proportion of crabmeat used contributes greatly to the taste, and the quality of crabmeat used also is very important. It follows naturally, therefore, that a deviled crab made from the Backfin Lump, the highest priced meat, will be tastiest. For less expensive tastes, we suggest the clawmeat.

Deviled crab baking shells, $5.00 each
Set of six in box, $45.00

Baker, whitefish $20.00
Bakers, shells, individual . . . . .$4.00 each
Set in box $45.00

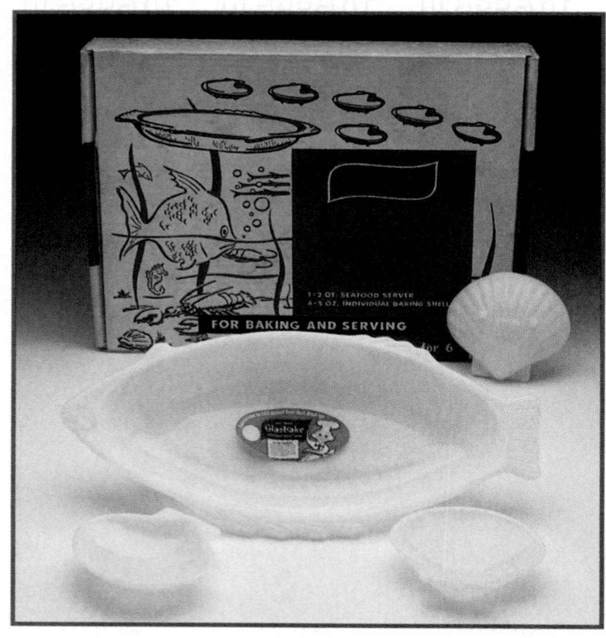

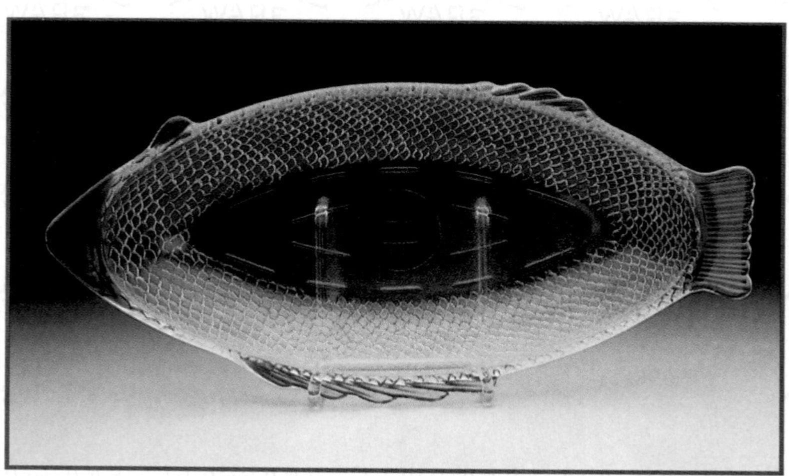

Crystal fish baker, 17" nose to tail, $16.00

Miscellaneous

Row 1:

Refrigerator dish, 9" x 5" $22.00
Custard, J2409 . . . .$8.00
Baker, 5¼" x 7⅞" $20.00

Row 2:

Baker/fridge, 5¼" x 7⅞", Maid of Honor . .$20.00
Refrigerator dish, J258-21, 4½" x 5" $12.00
Baker/fridge, 5¼" x 7⅞" $15.00

Row 3:

Baker, J2352, 2½ qt., divided $15.00
Baker/server, J2352, 2½ qt., divided $10.00

McKee mixing bowls
9" $25.00
8" $20.00
7" $15.00
6" $10.00

McKee "Chicken" mixing bowl, 8", $30.00.

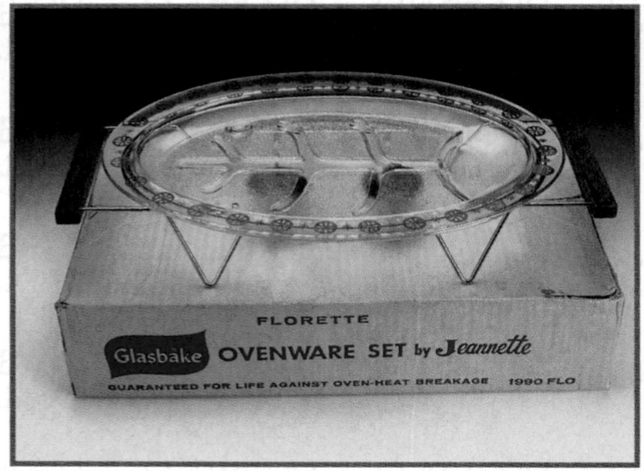

Florette platter, Well & Tree, $8.00
In rack, $12.00
In box, $18.00

Flamex saucepan or skillet, 8", $15.00

Skillet or saucepan, 10⅛", $20.00

Hottles, $8.00 each

White hottle, $12.00

McKee hottle, with yellow, $10.00

Measuring cup, 8 oz., 3½" high, $15.00

Cereal bowl, J2401, 6", $6.00

Mixmaster set	
Small bowl, 6⅞"	$18.00
Large bowl, 9⅜"	$22.00
Complete set	$60.00
with book	$70.00

Mixmaster set	
Bowls, 6⅞" wide	$20.00 each
Bowl, 9⅜" wide	$25.00
Set, with two bowls	$65.00

Comparison of company mugs	
Fire-King, 3⅜"	$12.00
Glasbake, J2402, 3⅜"	$10.00
Federal, 3⅜"	$8.00

Comparison of company mugs, same pattern	
Hazel-Atlas, 3⅜"	$12.00
Glasbake, 3¼", 2⁵⁄₁₆" rim bottom	$12.00

Item	Price
Basketweave, J2277	$12.00
Soup	$6.00
Basketweave, J2277	$12.00
Square, J2267, 3⅝"	$6.00
White with diamonds	$10.00

Lemons, $6.00
Oranges, $6.00

Top row:		**Bottom row:**	
Golf	$12.00	Flowers	$6.00
Baseball	$12.00	Basketweave	$12.00
Astronaut	$15.00	Basketweave	$12.00
Dyn-O-Mite	$8.00	"Soup's on"	$6.00
Children's	$12.00	Basketweave	$12.00
Children's	$12.00	Basketweave	$12.00
		Grape, Cherry	$6.00 each

Top row:		**Bottom row:**	
Kitten	$12.00	"Grandpa"	$8.00
Flowers	$8.00 each	Winter scene	$8.00
Middle row:		Red	$5.00
Butterfly	$10.00	Vegetables	$6.00
Owls	$12.00 each	Yellow striped	$6.00
Panda	$12.00		

Front views

Back views

Row 1:
All Language of Flowers . . . . .$10.00 each

Row 2:
Language of Flowers$10.00
Golf $12.00
Bowling $12.00
Sunbonnet $12.00

Row 3:
Sunbonnet $12.00
Sunbonnet $12.00
Children $12.00

Row 1:
Orphan Annie $15.00
Comic . . . .$10.00 each

Row 2:
Advertising $8.00
Advertising $8.00
Bicentennial $12.00
Bicentennial $12.00

Row 3:
All advertising . . . .$8.00 each

Comic, $10.00

Glasbake & Range-tec

Row 1:
- Double boiler, Cory $25.00
- Coffee server/warmer, silver rings, McKee $30.00
- Coffee pot, pastel rings . .$35.00

Row 2:
- Teapot, McKee Range-tec $25.00
- Teapot, pastel rings, Glasbake $35.00
- Dish, 5" x 4¼", yellowish cast $15.00
- Refrigerator dish, 4" x 4" $15.00

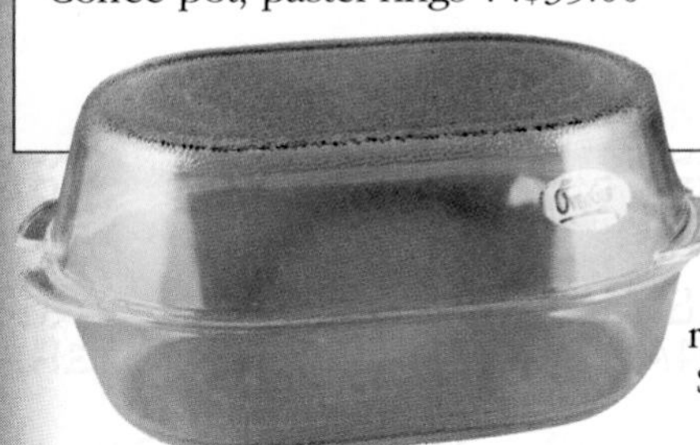

Large roaster, $60.00

McKee Range-tec skillet or saucepan, 8⅜", $15.00
McKee Range-tec skillet or saucepan, 7⅛", $12.00

heat resistant
Glasbake®
OVENWARE RANGEWARE PATIOWARE

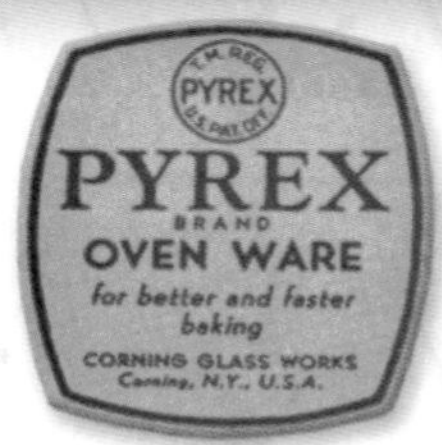

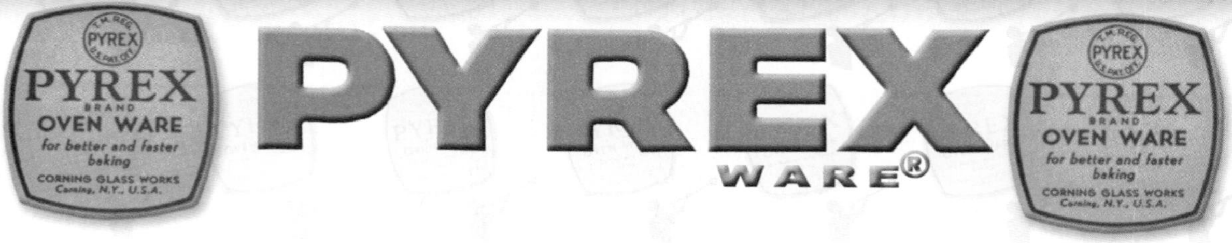
PYREX
OVEN WARE
for better and faster baking
CORNING GLASS WORKS
Corning, N.Y., U.S.A.
PYREX
WARE®
PYREX
OVEN WARE
for better and faster baking
CORNING GLASS WORKS
Corning, N.Y., U.S.A.

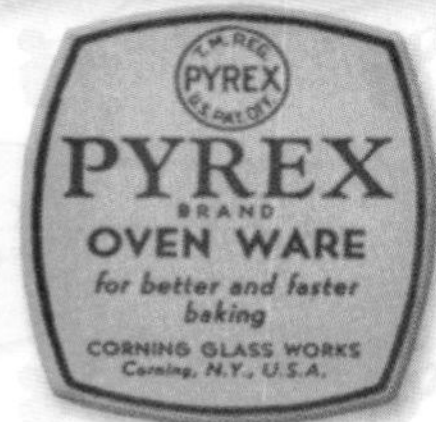

PYREX
Division of Corning Glass Corporation, 1917 – Present

As with Fire-King, all of us grew up seeing Pyrex being used by our moms or grandmothers. The Pyrex four-color mixing bowl set is as recognized as Fire-King's Jade-ite or Sapphire blue ovenware. Those colored mixing bowls were made for over 30 years, but finding mint condition ones is not easy, as they were heavily used in most homes. Many Pyrex items are labeled "Not for stove top or broiler."

The red "Tulip" decoration on crystal ovenware from the 1930s is a most elusive and desired pattern by collectors, but Pink and Turquoise with or without white decorations sell even faster due to a more abundant supply available from the 1950s.

Later-issued Pyrex is usually marked for "Oven or Microwave use."

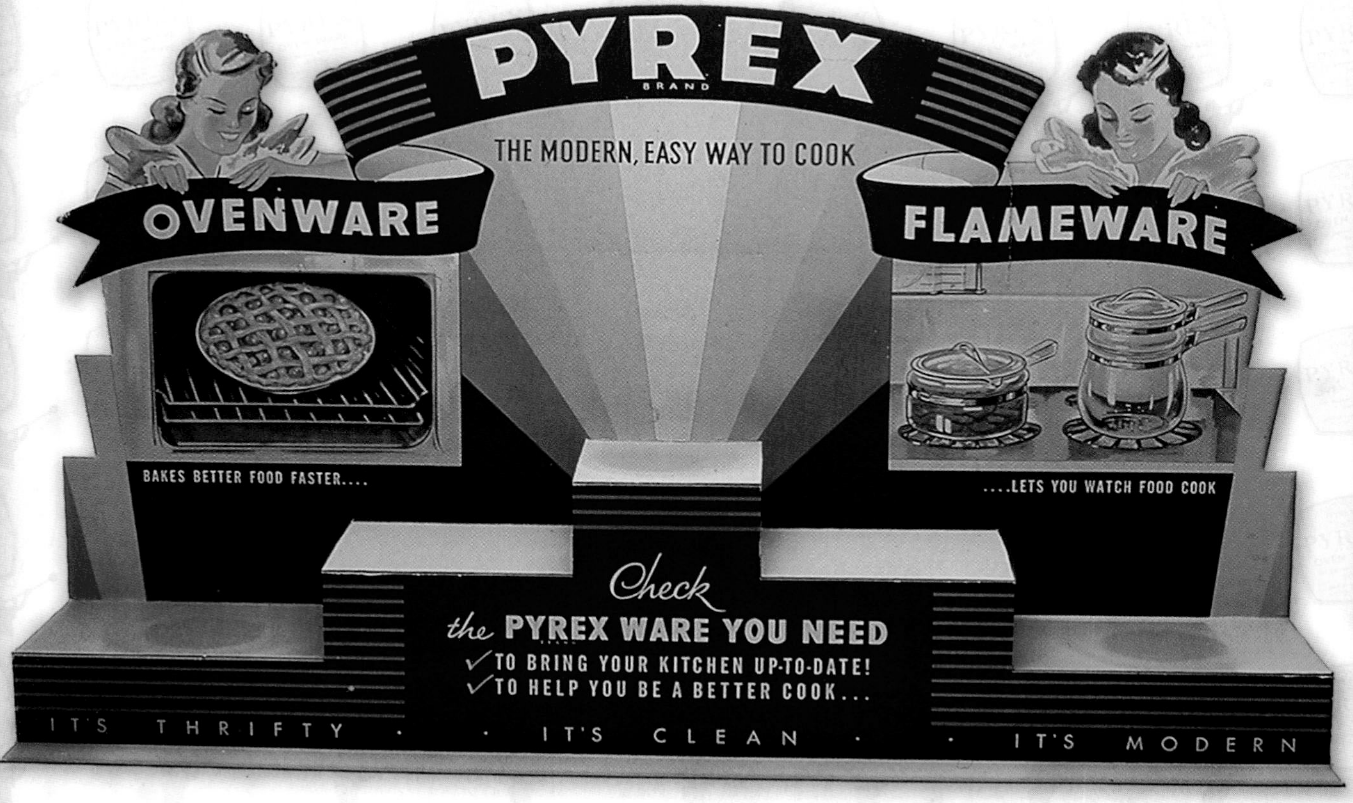
PYREX
BRAND
THE MODERN, EASY WAY TO COOK
OVENWARE
FLAMEWARE
BAKES BETTER FOOD FASTER....
....LETS YOU WATCH FOOD COOK
Check
the PYREX WARE YOU NEED
✓TO BRING YOUR KITCHEN UP-TO-DATE!
✓TO HELP YOU BE A BETTER COOK...
IT'S THRIFTY · · IT'S CLEAN · · IT'S MODERN

a product of Corning Glass Works, Corning, N.Y.

Custard cups
Set of four, 5 oz. .$5.00 each
Set in box $35.00

Economy Set, nine piece	
Measuring cup	$10.00
Custard cups	$4.00 each
Plate	$8.00
Set in box	$60.00

"HANDI-KIT" SET

No.	Pieces in Set	Sets in Case	Weight Case Lbs.	Retail Price Per Set
445	6	12	19	$ .39

6—5-oz. Dainty Custard Cups, newest rimless style, for oven baking and table serving of custards, desserts, souffles and popovers. Gift packaged.

Any woman can find a need for these every time she turns around. For baking, serving and storing.

GRAND GIFT FOR SHOWERS

Announcing redesigned

PYREX

SE

... For

CUSTARD CUP SET

No.	Pieces in Set	Sets in Case	Weight Case Lbs.	Retail Price Per Set
59	7	12	25	$ .59

6—5-oz. Dainty Custard Cups and a Handy Wire Rack for convenience in baking, serving and storing of desserts, custards, etc. Gift boxed.

They're good-looking, useful and fast-selling. Six custard cups and a wire rack for easy handling.

14

9-PIECE "ECONOMY" SET

No.	Pieces in Set	Sets in Case	Weight Case Lbs.	Retail Price Per Set
179	9	6	30	$ .79

Contents: 1 each 9½" Pie Plate, 8-oz. level-full Measuring Cup with permanent red graduations, and six 4-oz. Custard Cups with handy Wire Rack.

This new 9-piece Ovenware set is a grand start for cooking in glass. Packed in attractive new gift display box.

the completely line of . . .

WARE

TS

1940

BIRTHDAY S . . . PARTIES . . . XMAS

8-PIECE MATCHED SET

No.	Pieces in Set	Sets in Case	Weight Case Lbs.	Retail Price Per Set
145	8	6	34	$1.00

Contents: 1—1½ qt. Casserole with Pie Plate Cover, and 6—5 oz. Dainty Custard Cups, in matched design in an attractive gift box.

They match! The six thin custard cups repeat the design of the attractive covered casserole.

15

10-PIECE "SERVICE" SET

No.	Pieces in Set	Sets in Case	Weight Case Lbs.	Price Per Set Retail
129	10	6	46	$1.29

CONTENTS

1—8 oz. Level-Full Measuring Cup with permanent red graduations
1—9½" Pie Plate
1—1½ qt. Casserole (2 pc.)
Pie Plate Cover
6—4 oz. Custard Cups

Spring special with 10 selected Pyrex dishes. Value of individual pieces, $1.35. Packed in smart gift container.

EVERY PIECE OF PYREX WARE BACK

11-PIECE GIFT SET

No.	Pieces in Set	Sets in Case	Weight Case Lbs.	Retail Price Per Set	Retail Price E-2 Eng.
245	11	1	15	$2.45	$4.95

CONTENTS

1—1½ qt. Casserole
1—10½" Utility Dish
1—9½" Pie Plate
1—9⅛" Loaf Pan
6—4 oz. Custard Cups
1—8⅝" Cake Dish with handles

Packed in Silver and Blue gift box —a lovely wedding present.

Women will love this useful set. Eleven pieces—including the serviceable round cake dish with handles.

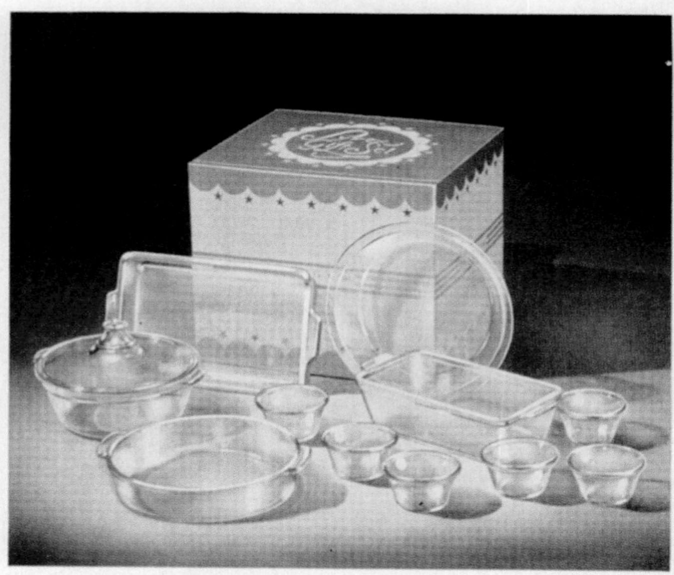

16

17-PIECE "HOME BAKER" SET

No.	Pieces in Set	Sets in Case	Weight Case Lbs.	Retail Price Per Set
295	17	1	20	$2.95

CONTENTS

1—8 oz. Level-Full Measuring Cup with permanent red graduations
1—12⅝" Utility Dish
1—9⅛" Loaf Pan
1—9½" Pie Plate
2—8⅝" Cake Dishes
4—8 oz. Individual Deep Pie Dishes
6—4 oz. Custard Cups
1—Handy Wire Rack

Here's a set designed to meet 90% of a housewife's baking needs. Seventeen pieces packed in a gift display box.

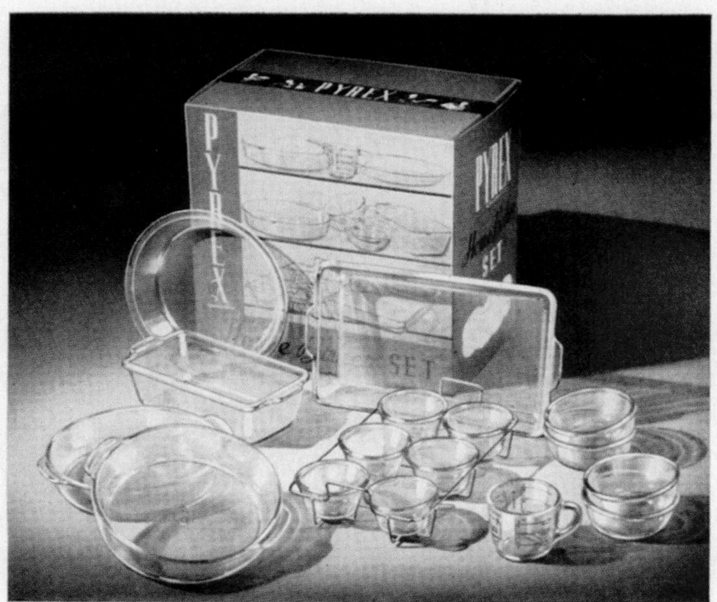

ED BY FAMOUS REPLACEMENT OFFER

PYREX WARE SETS...THE IDEAL GIFT!

Today, more than ever, Pyrex ware *sets* are ideal for weddings, anniversaries, showers, birthdays, bridge parties—any gift occasion!

Attractively packaged and gift-wrapped, this gleaming ware wins any woman's heart. And all items are carefully selected by home economists from the famous Corning Test Kitchen, so that every set, no matter how small, finds a practical place in the modern kitchen.

The Pyrex ware line of sets for 1940 has been completely redesigned. New, carefully thought-out combinations . . . lovely new packages . . . and in many cases new savings, make them more popular than ever for promotion. Combined with the 30% to 50% price reduction of less than two years ago, it means that Pyrex ware—in sets—is now well within the reach of everyone.

And don't forget—Pyrex ware in sets is the ideal way for any woman to start her *own* kitchen outfit! Beginning with one of the smaller standard sets, she may gradually add extra items until she has at last a piece to meet any household requirement!

To start, to save, to give—it's *Pyrex ware in SETS* for 1940!

17

IT'S EASIER TO BE A BETTER COOK

CASSEROLES—ROUND—KNOB COVER

No.	U. S. Trade Size	Outside Dimensions in Inches	Pieces in Case	Weight Case Lbs.	Retail Price Each	Price Engraved Each
621	½ qt.	6 x2¼	12	23	$ .40	$ .85
622	1 qt.	6⅞x2¾	12	30	.50	1.00
623	1½ qt.	7⅞x3	12	34	.65	1.20
624	2 qt.	8⅞x3¼	12	51	.75	1.45

DOUBLE DUTY CASSEROLES—ROUND—UTILITY COVER

No.	U. S. Trade Size	Outside Dimensions in Inches	Pieces in Case	Weight Case Lbs.	Retail Price Each	Price Engraved Each
682	1 qt.	6⅞x2¾	12	34	$ .50	$1.00
683	1½ qt.	7⅞x3	12	40	.65	1.20
684	2 qt.	8⅞x3¼	12	55	.75	1.45
686	3 qt.	10⅜x3½	6	38	.95	1.65

CASSEROLES—OVAL—DEEP

No.	U. S. Trade Size	Outside Dimensions in Inches	Pieces in Case	Weight Case Lbs.	Retail Price Each	Price Engraved Each
632	1 qt.	8 x5⅞x2⅞	12	32	$ .50	$1.00
633	1½ qt.	9⅛x6⅝x3	12	42	.65	1.20
634	2 qt.	10⅛x7½x3¼	12	54	.75	1.45

OPEN BAKERS—ROUND

No.	U. S. Trade Size	Outside Dimensions in Inches	Pieces in Case	Weight Case Lbs.	Retail Price Each	Price Engraved Each
021	½ qt.	6 x2¼	12	15	$ .25	$ .55
022	1 qt.	6⅞x2¾	12	19	.35	.65
023	1½ qt.	7⅞x3	12	21	.45	.80
024	2 qt.	8⅞x3¼	12	37	.55	.95
026	3 qt.	10⅜x3½	6	27	.65	1.10

These bakers are bottom parts of corresponding round casseroles.

REPLACEMENT OFFER

Any dish or part of PYREX brand Ovenware which breaks from oven-heat within two years from date of purchase, may be replaced by any dealer in PYREX brand Ware *in exchange* for the broken pieces.

2

Matched Set	
Custard cups	$4.00 each
Casserole	$12.00
Set in box	$50.00

Gift Set

Top row:		Bottom row:	
Custard cups	$4.00 each	Casserole	$12.00
Casserole	$12.00	Baking dish	$12.00
		Loaf pan	$8.00
Set in box			$80.00

Engraved Ware

STYLE E-2

Attractive engraved design available on 21 pieces.

No.	Description	Retail Price
81E-2	1 Cup Engraved Teapot—Glass Lock-on Cover and Ebony Black Handle	$1.35
81E-2	Engraved Teapot Bowl only	.85
84E-2	6 Cup Engraved Teapot—Glass Lock-on Cover and Ebony Black Handle	1.95
84E-2	Engraved Teapot Bowl only	1.20
209E-2	9½" Engraved Pie Plate—Round	.55
212E-2	9⅛" Engraved Bread or Loaf Pan—Oblong	.80
221E-2	8⅝" Cake Dish—Round	.60
231E-2	10½" Engraved Utility Dish—Oblong	.90
232E-2	12⅝" Engraved Utility Dish—Oblong	1.15
316E-2	15" Engraved Platter—Oval	2.50
372E-2	15" Engraved Well and Tree Platter	2.35
414E-2	4 oz. Engraved Custard Cups—Round—Shallow	.15
453E-2	8 oz. Engraved Individual Deep Pie Dishes—Round	.25
455E-2	12 oz. Engraved Individual Deep Pie Dishes—Round	.30
622E-2	1 qt. Engraved Casserole—Round—Knob Cover	1.00
623E-2	1½ qt. Engraved Casserole—Round—Knob Cover	1.20
624E-2	2 qt. Engraved Casserole—Round—Knob Cover	1.45
632E-2	1 qt. Engraved Casserole—Oval—Knob Cover	1.00
633E-2	1½ qt. Engraved Casserole—Oval—Knob Cover	1.20
634E-2	2 qt. Engraved Casserole—Oval—Knob Cover	1.45
683E-2	1½ qt. Engraved Casserole—Round—Utility Cover	1.20
684E-2	2 qt. Engraved Casserole—Round—Utility Cover	1.45
686E-2	3 qt. Engraved Casserole—Round—Utility Cover	1.65

ENGRAVED GIFT SET

No.	Description	Retail Price
245E-2	11 piece Engraved Gift Set	4.95

For Data on Packing and Weight See Corresponding Items in Plain PYREX Ware.

Designed to bake perfectly, this beautiful engraved casserole also adds a distinctive touch to the dinner table.

WILL NOT TRANSFER FLAVORS

Casseroles With Engraved Covers Only

STYLE E-7

(Plain Bodies)

Engraved custard, 4 oz., $8.00

7

Engraved pie dish, 8 oz., $15.00

Pyrex

JUST look at the sparkling modern Pyrex ware on these shelves! Every dish has a triple use—for cooking, serving, and storing. Don't wait! Stop at your favorite store now and get the Pyrex ware you need at today's low prices.

1 **PIE PLATE.** Fast-baking Pyrex brand pie plate turns out "picture" pies every time. Four sizes—8½" pie plate only . . . 20¢

2 **CUSTARD CUPS.** Deep, 5 ounce custard cups for individual puddings, custards, popovers. You'll surely want a dozen! Each . . 5¢

3 **LOAF PAN.** This loaf pan bakes bread, fish, meat, desserts, and keeps them hot! Two sizes. 9⅛" size only . . . . 45¢

4 **ROUND KNOB-COVER CASSEROLE.** Keeps food hot for second servings. 5 sizes. Convenient quart size only . . . . 50¢

5 **DOUBLE BOILER.** Get a Pyrex double boiler. Watch food come to just the right consistency! Two sizes; quart size only $3.45

6 **MEASURING CUP.** Red-marked for easy measuring. Comes in three handy sizes . . . 8-oz., 16-oz., and 32-oz. 8-oz. size only . . . . . 15¢

7 **SAUCEPAN.** Wide flat bottoms "fit" top burners, speed up cooking. Sticky foods wash off easily. 1 quart size only $1.65

8 **WELL AND TREE PLATTER.** Get it piping hot in the oven for serving broiled steaks. Well catches healthful meat juices. Only $1.85

9 **EIGHT-PIECE MATCHED SET.** 1½ quart casserole with pie plate cover and six 5-oz. matching custard cups. Gift boxed $1.00

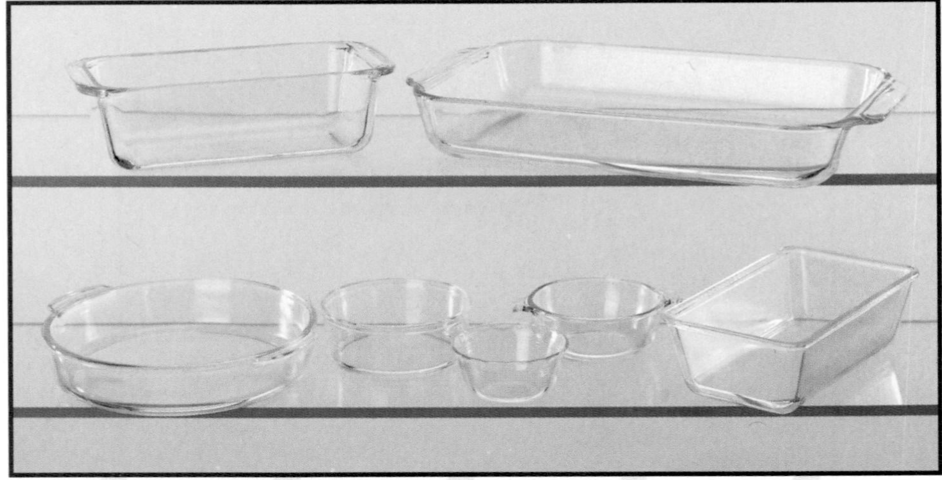

Top row:	
Loaf pan $10.00	Custard, 4 oz. $4.00
Utility dish, 10½" $12.00	Baker, 8 oz. $5.00
Bottom row:	Bread or loaf pan $10.00
Cake dish, 8⅝", with handles . .$12.00	
Pie plate, 8 oz., deep $7.00	

Circa 1920s bean pot, 506, 2 qt., $22.00

Utility dish in holder, $22.00
Casserole in holder, 1½ qt., $25.00

Windmill & Dutch girl design casserole, with lid, $45.00

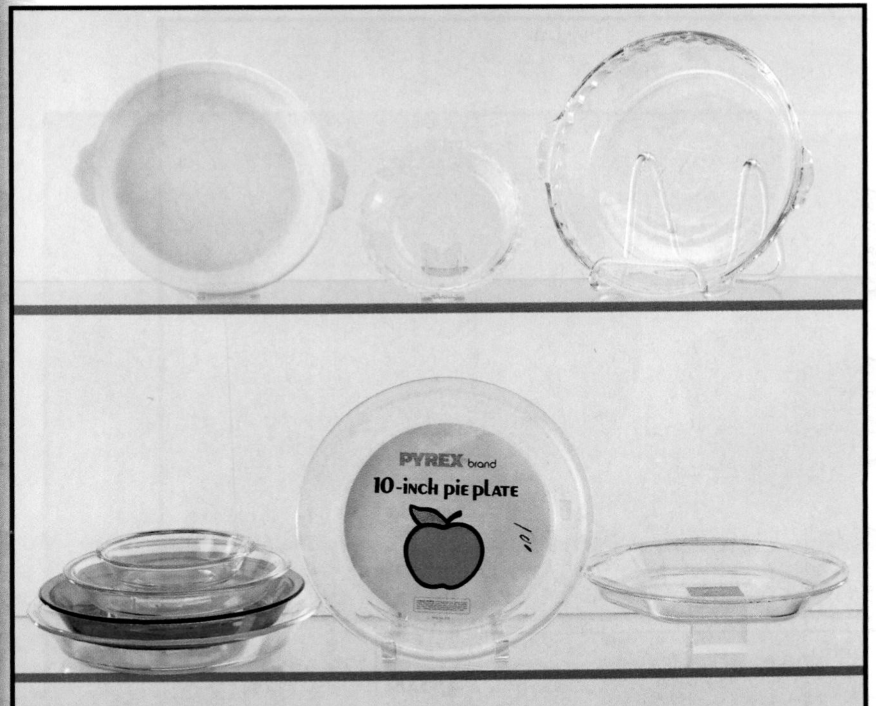

Top row:

Item	Price
Cake dish, 9", with handles	$12.00
Baker, 6⅛"	$5.00
"Flavor Saver," 10", 75th Anniversary	$8.00

Bottom row:

Item	Price
Pie plates	
11"	$9.00
9⅞", cobalt	$5.00
8½"	$6.00
6"	$4.00
Pie plate, 10"	$3.00
Pie plate, #1203, 9⅞", hexagonal	$15.00

Colors – *Lime*

Top row:		**Bottom row:**	
Dish, 1½ qt., baking, tab handles	$12.00	Casserole, 1½ qt., 8½", round	$20.00
Loaf pan, 1½ qt.	$15.00	Utility dish, 2qt.	$18.00
Baker, 2 qt., 8¼", round	$15.00		

Square cake dish, 8", $15.00
Individual covered casserole, 8 oz., $12.00

Colors – *Desert Yellow & Turquoise*

Baker, 1½ qt., 8¼", round	$25.00
Baker (top), oval	$20.00
Baker (bottom), oval	$25.00
Lid, divided only	$10.00
Baker, 1½ pt., individual	$12.00

Colors – *Turquoise*

Bowls, mixing
- 4 qt. $30.00
- 2½ qt. $20.00
- 1½ qt. $15.00
- 1½ pt. $12.00
- Set of four $70.00

Colors – *Pink*

Top row:

Oven-refrigerator dishes, with lids
- 1½ cup $15.00
- 1½ qt. $22.00
- 1½ pt. $18.00
- 1½ cup $15.00
- Set of three, with lids $55.00

Bottom row:
- Bowl, 1½ qt., mixing $15.00
- Bowl, 4 qt., mixing $35.00

Mother's Day Gifts...for June Brides, too!

Give time-saving **PYREX**® *ware!*

• PYREX Color Bowl Set for mixing, oven baking, and storing. Four bowls—all in smart, new turquoise, pink, and assorted colors—$2.95

HERE'S A QUICK AND EASY WAY to solve your gift problems for Mother's Day, bridal showers and weddings. Choose smart, exciting PYREX ware to more than please any woman on your list. Look over the items on this page—see all the other PYREX ware gift suggestions at your nearest dealer's!

• PYREX Oven-Refrigerator-Freezer Set. So handy so many ways! Lids can be used as hot pads, trays or platters. Four dishes—in new pink, turquoise, or assorted colors—$3.45

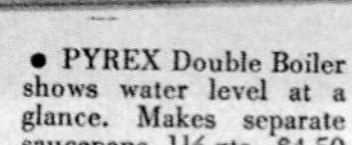

• PYREX Teapot for boiling, brewing and serving. Beautifully graceful. 6-cup capacity, $2.50

• PYREX Double Boiler shows water level at a glance. Makes separate saucepans. 1½ qts., $4.50

• PYREX Percolator gives you clean, pure coffee flavor every time, even when reheated. 6-cup, $3.95

• PYREX Casserole. Freeze, cook, serve, store in same dish. Yellow, Pink, Turquoise. 2-qt., $1.75

• PYREX Mixing Bowl Set for mixing, baking, and many other kitchen uses. Set of 3, only $1.50

• PYREX Dinnerware. 16-piece set—choice of colors—$6.95 (Borders banded in gold, $9.95)

PYREX ware is the star of the cooking world. Look for it on TV, in magazines, everywhere. See what's cooking!

There's only one PYREX BRAND Ware, a product of  CORNING GLASS WORKS, Corning, N.Y.

VISIT THE CORNING GLASS CENTER, CORNING, N.Y.

"PYREX" is a registered trademark in the U.S. of Corning Glass Works, Corning, N.Y.

Top row:		**Bottom row:**	
Bowls, mixing		Oven-refrigerator dishes, with lids	
4 qt.	$20.00	1½ cup	$10.00
1½ qt.	$10.00	1½ qt.	$15.00
1½ pt.	$10.00	1½ pt.	$12.00
2½ qt.	$12.50	1½ cup	$10.00

Note two styles of bottoms on mixing bowls. Earlier bowls were advertised as ½ qt., 1¼ qt., 2¾ qt., 4 qt.

Ramekin, 7 oz., $8.00

Hostess casserole, 1½ qt., $25.00
Without lid, $12.50

Handy Double-Duty Casserole—bottom makes an open baker. Cover is an extra pie plate. 1 to 3 qt. sizes, as low as **60¢** and up.

All-glass PYREX Percolators make grand coffee! Hard to find now, but worth looking for. 6-cup size, only **$2.95.**

Gleaming PYREX Utility Dish is just right for small roasts, chops, hot breads, cakes. Two sizes, only **50¢** and **75¢.**

Use Two PYREX Cake Dishes for perfect layer cakes. Also as small roaster. With handles. Only **45¢** each.

Famous PYREX Flameware Set—7" skillet, 1 and 1½ quart saucepans with detachable handle, only **$2.45**. Cover, **30¢** extra.

Special Knob Cover Casserole cooks foods 1/3 faster, is lovely for serving. Round shape, four sizes from **60¢** up.

If Dad goes for nut bread, baked salmon, scalloped oysters or home baked beans, you'll go for the PYREX Loaf Pan. Two sizes: **50¢, 75¢.**

1 pt. Measuring Cup with easy-to-read, lifetime red markings. Resists heat and acids. Special smooth-pouring spout. Only **50¢.**

Flavor-Saver Pie Plate bakes pies better. Fluted edges, extra depth keep juices *inside!* Easy-to-hold handles. 10" size, only **50¢.**

T.M. REG.
PYREX
U.S. PAT. OFF.

PYREX
BRAND
OVEN WARE
for better and faster baking
CORNING GLASS WORKS
Corning, N.Y., U.S.A.

Newly designed dishes for custards, popovers, individual soufflés, deep pies. 6, 9, 15 oz. sizes—only **5¢-10¢-15¢** each.

Watch pies cook evenly in this smart PYREX pie plate. Sticky foods wash off like magic. Three sizes—**25¢-30¢-35¢.**

THERE'S ONLY ONE PYREX WARE AND IT'S MADE BY CORNING GLASS

Set of 4 nested PYREX Color Bowls, heat resistant and 2½ times stronger than ordinary bowls. ¾, 1½, 2½, 4 qt. bowls, complete **$2.95.**

Crystal-Clear Nested PYREX Bowl Set—for mixing, baking, serving and storing. Also for salads, desserts. 1, 1½, 2½ qt. bowls, complete **$1.00.**

OB

Ever dream there were so many lovely Pyrex Dishes?

Pyrex

Colors – *Blue, Green, Yellow*

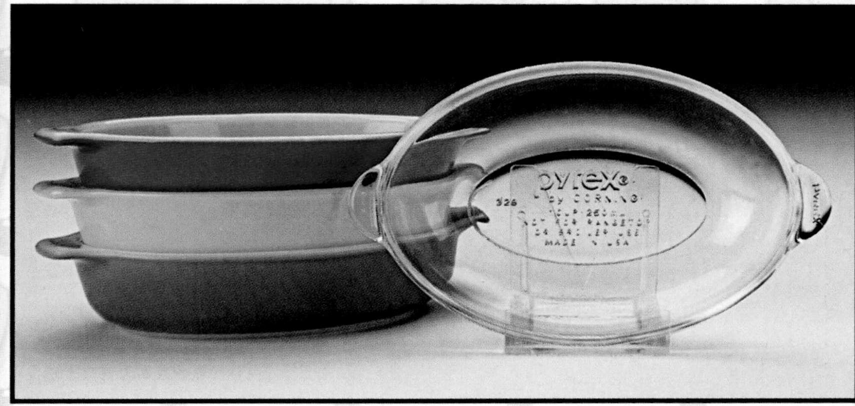

Pixie casseroles, 7 oz., $10.00 each
Casserole, 7 oz., with lid, $14.00

Colors – *Browns*

Bowl, 1½ pt., mixing $8.00
Oven-refrigerator dish,
1½ cup, with lid $10.00
Oven-refrigerator dish,
1½ cup, with lid $10.00

Colors – *Yellow*

Pie plate, yellow, $14.00

Festive meals can be so easy!

New PYREX Golden Casserole goes from oven to table in its own gleaming cradle. And twin candle warmers keep food hot for second servings. Use the clear glass cover as an extra serving dish. 2½-qt., **$6.95** PYREX Carafe with candle warmer keeps any beverage steaming hot, never borrows flavors. 12-cup, $4.95; 8-cup, **$3.95**

Right: PYREX Bake-Serve-and-Store Set in turquoise or pink, with clear lids, easy-grip handles. All wash clean in a twinkling! Set **$3.95**

PYREX® WARE *a symbol of modern living, is a product of* **CORNING** *research*

Advertisement c. 1959

Bowls, mixing		Refrigerator dishes, with lids	
4 qt.	$12.00	1½ pt.	$10.00
2½ qt.	$10.00	1½ cup	$8.00
1½ qt.	$8.00		

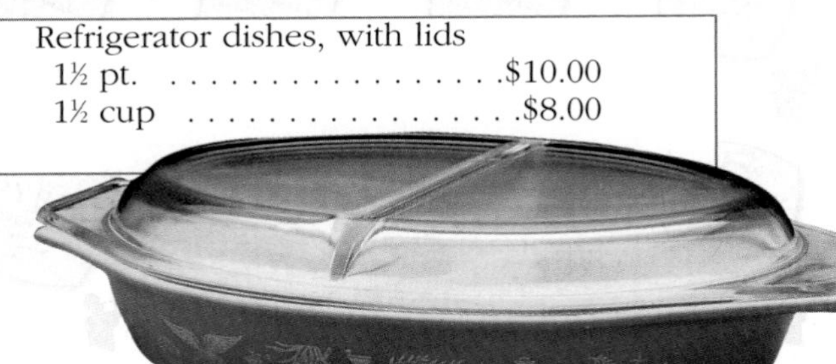

Divided dish, 1½ qt., $22.00

Patterns – *Americana*

Bowl, 1½ pt., $12.00

Patterns – *"Arches"*

Casserole, 1½ qt., $12.50

Patterns – *Autumn Harvest*

Top row:
Bowls, mixing
1½ pt. $8.00
2½ qt. $12.00

Bottom row:
Bowls, mixing
1½ pt. $8.00
4 qt. $12.00
1½ qt. $10.00

Patterns – *"Balloons"*

Cinderella bowl,
4 qt., 9¾", $15.00

Top row:	
Bake/serve/store casseroles	
1 pt.	$10.00
1½ pt.	$10.00
Cinderella bowl, 4 qt., mixing	$14.00
Cinderella bowl, 2½ qt., mixing	$12.00
Cinderella bowl, 1½ pt., mixing	$8.00
Bake/serve/store casseroles	
1½ qt.	$14.00
1 qt.	$12.00
Bottom row:	
Butter dish, ¼ lb.	$12.00
Butter dish, ¼ lb.	$12.00
Utility dish, 3 qt.	$18.00

Item	Price
Butter dish, ¼ lb.	$12.00
Sugar	$5.00
Creamer	$5.00

Cinderella bowls	
2½ qt.	$12.00
1½ pt.	$8.00
1½ qt.	$10.00
4 qt.	$15.00
Set	$45.00

Top row:

Cinderella bake/serve/store, set #470

- 1 qt. $16.00
- 1½ pt. $14.00
- 1 pt. $12.00

Cinderella bowls, set #470

- 4 qt. $16.00
- 2½ qt. $14.00
- 1½ qt. $12.00
- 1½ pt. $10.00

Bottom row:

- Bowl, 1½ pt., mixing $10.00
- Oven-refrigerator dish, 1½ qt. $18.00
- Oven-refrigerator dish, 1½ pt $10.00
- Oven-refrigerator dish, 1½ pt. $10.00
- Butter dish, #72 . . . . $12.00

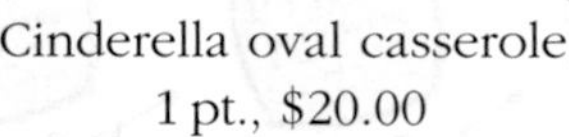

Cinderella oval casserole,
1 pt., $20.00

Cinderella bowl, 4 qt. $12.00
Lid $3.00
Casserole, 1½ qt. $15.00

Cinderella bowl, 4 qt., $12.00
Casserole, 2½ qt., $14.00

Mixing bowl, 1½ qt., $9.00

Patterns – *Daisy*

Top row:
- Casserole, 2½ qt. $25.00
- Oven-refrigerator dish, 1½ cup $10.00
- Utility dish, 3 qt., rectangular $18.00

Bottom row:
Bake/serve/store casseroles
- 1½ pt. $22.00
- 2½ qt. $25.00
- 1 pt. $20.00

Casserole, 2½ qt.,
$25.00

Cinderella oval divided dish, 1½ qt., $18.00
In box, $22.00

Patterns – *Empire Scroll*

Casserole, 1½ qt., $12.00

Patterns – *Friendship*

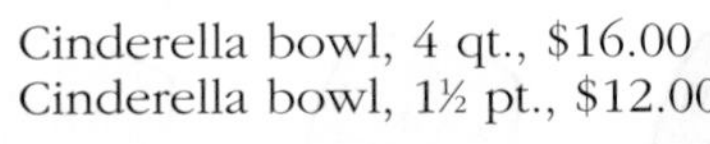

Cinderella bowl, 4 qt., $16.00
Cinderella bowl, 1½ pt., $12.00

Patterns – *Forest Fancies*

Mixing bowl,
1½ qt., $10.00

Patterns – *Golden Acorn,* *c. 1960s*

Oval decorator casserole, 1½ qt., $20.00
Divided serving dish, #963, 1½ qt., $16.00

Patterns – *"Golden Hearts,"* *c. late 1950s*

Casserole, 2½ qt., with warmer, $22.00

Patterns – *Golden Honeysuckle,* *c. 1960s*

Oblong casserole, #935, 2½ qt., $18.00

Patterns – *Golden Scroll*

Cinderella bowls
- 4 qt. $12.00
- 2 qt. $12.00
- 1½ pt. $8.00

Patterns – *Gooseberry*

Cinderella bowls
- 4 qt. $15.00
- 2½ qt. $14.00
- 1½ qt. $13.00
- 1½ pt. $12.00

Top row:

Oven-refrigerator dish, 1½ cup . . .$10.00

Bake/serve/store casseroles
- 2½ qt. $16.00
- 1½ pt. $12.00

Oven-refrigerator dish, 1½ pt. $12.00

Bottom row:

Cinderella bowls
- 1½ qt. $16.00
- 4 qt. $18.00
- 1½ pt. $12.00

Patterns – *"Grapevine,"* *c. early 1960s*

Chip and dip set, #64, $20.00

Patterns – *Homestead*

Bowls, mixing, #300
2½ qt. $12.00
1½ qt. $10.00
1½ pt. $8.00

Patterns – *Horizon*

Cinderella bowls set #440
4 qt. $14.00
2½ qt. $14.00
1½ qt. $10.00
1½ pt. $12.00

Casserole, 1 qt., $14.00
Casserole, 1½ pt., $12.00

Bowls, mixing (left to right)

1½ qt.	$8.00
2½ qt.	$10.00
1½ pt.	$8.00
4 qt.	$10.00
1½ qt.	$8.00

Casserole, 1 qt., $12.00
With holder, $18.00

Cinderella casserole, 1½ qt., divided server, w/cover	$18.00
Cinderella casserole, #963, 1½ qt., divided, w/cover	$18.00
Casserole, #943, 1½ qt., oval	$18.00
Cinderella casserole, #963, 1½ qt., divided, w/cover	$20.00
Sauce boat and liner, English mark	$20.00

Rectangular brown space saver casserole, #575, 2 qt., $15.00
Rectangular turquoise space saver casserole, #575, 2 qt., $20.00

Top row:
Bake/store/serve
Casserole, 1½ pt. $10.00
Casserole, 1 qt. $12.00
Cinderella bowls
4 qt., mixing $10.00
2½ qt., mixing $10.00
Bake/store/serve
Casserole, 1 qt. $8.00
Casserole, 1 pt. $10.00

Bottom row:
Oven-refrigerator dish, 1½ pt. $12.00
Casserole, #924, 2 qt. $12.00
Butter dish, #72, ¼ lb. $12.00

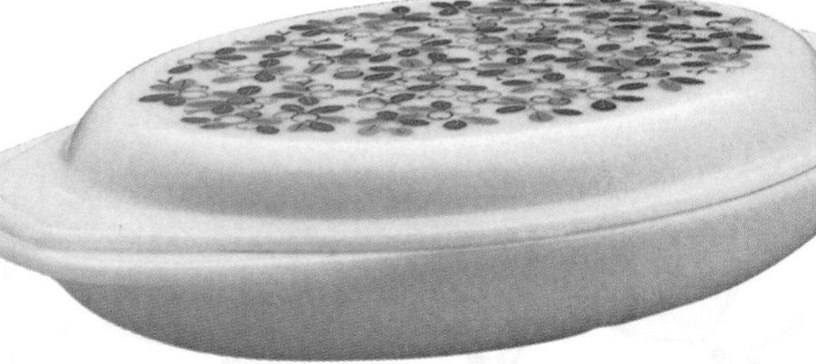

Casserole, 1½ qt., $15.00

Pair of shakers, $8.00
Butter dish, $12.00

Patterns – *Terra*, *c. mid-1960s (short production)*

Back row:		Front row:	
Casserole, 2½ qt.	$12.00	Bowl, 10 oz.	$5.00
Bowl, 4 qt.	$10.00	Bowl, 1½ pt.	$6.00
Bowl, 2½ qt.	$8.00	Plate, 9⅜"	$4.00
Casserole, 1½ qt.	$10.00	Mug, 12 oz., 3½"	$5.00

PYREX®WARE

This is TERRA—a new trademark applied to a collection of homeware, timeless in its beauty . . . endless in its usefulness. This collection combines the classic elegance, the etched and textured feel and look of ancient handcrafted earthenware . . . with the contemporary freezer-to-oven-to-table convenience of today's PYREX® ware. It is just as useful as all PYREX ware has ever been in the kitchen—yet these practical pieces *could* be enjoyed *purely as decorative objects* in your home. The collection is completely flexible—just combine the pieces in any number you choose. Never has a collection of mugs and bowls and casseroles, plates and platters, given you so much toward easier, more attractive living—and at such sensible prices.

Exquisite for gracious entertaining

Just right for casual living, too

The perfect note to a Hawaiian Luau

Bowls
1½ pt., 2½ qt., 4 qt.

Casseroles
1 pt., 1½ pt., 1½ qt., 2½ qt.

Small Bowls
10 oz.

9" Plate

12" Plate

Mugs
12 oz.

TERRA: usefully beautiful. And remarkably, these exquisite pieces are perfect for everyday kitchen needs – for mixing, fixing, baking, storing, as well as serving. Like all PYREX ware, they are non-porous for easiest washing, and for freshest, best-tasting flavors! They make the meals you serve fit for a king . . . and the settings, in all the elegance of handcrafted earthenware, fit for a queen. This is the achievement called TERRA!

PYREX® WARE

a product of Corning

GUARANTEE: Any PYREX brand product which breaks from oven heat within two years of date of purchase, when used according to instructions, may be replaced by any PYREX ware dealer in exchange for the broken pieces.

LC-2678 Printed in U.S.A.

Pyrex

Patterns – *Town & Country,* c. mid-1960s

Cinderella bowl, 4 qt., $12.00

Divided casserole, 1½ qt., $15.00

Patterns – *Tulip,* c. 1930s

Square cake dish, #222, 8½", $75.00

Loaf pan, in holder, $55.00

Loaf pan, 5¼" x 10¼", $50.00

Patterns – *"Wheat"*

Bowl, 1½ qt., $9.00

Patterns – *Woodland*

Oval casserole, 1 qt., $12.00
Oven-refrigerator dish, 1½ pt., w/after '50s even-ridges top, $10.00

Oven-refrigerator dish, 1½ pt., $10.00
Casserole, 1½ pt., $12.00

Items – *Baster*

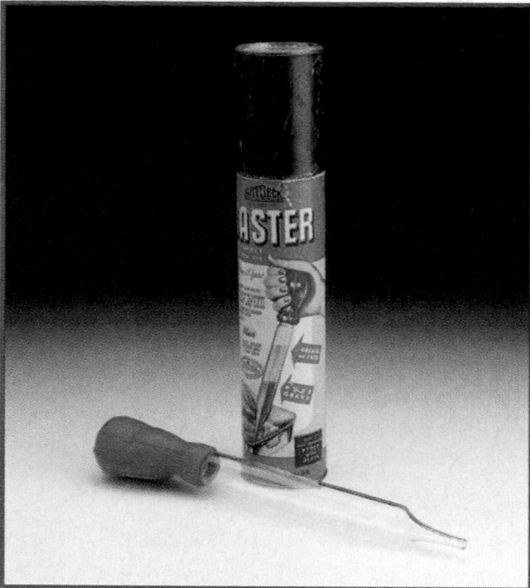

1946 Arodeck, $18.00

Items – *Bottles, Nursing*

4 oz., $12.00
8 oz., with box, $20.00

4 oz., 4¼"	$10.00
8 oz., 6⅝"	$15.00
4 oz., 4⅜"	$12.00

Pyrex

NEW. .4-ounce size: Mothers and doctors asked for this 4-ounce bottle—for baby's orange juice, drinking water, supplementary feedings, medicines or special foods. A great convenience in travelling. Narrow neck only

No.	Size	Price
54N	4 oz.	$ .15

REGULAR 8-OUNCE SIZE:

Narrow Neck			Wide Mouth		
No.	Size	Retail Price	No.	Size	Retail Price
58N	8 oz.	$ .30	**48W**	8 oz.	$ .30

Your Choice of Pyrex Nursing Bottles to Fit Each Feeding Need

Doctors all over the country urge the use of Pyrex Nursing Bottles because you can sterilize them hygienically clean in boiling water.

Risk of upsetting baby's schedule by bottle breakage at feeding time is virtually eliminated when you use Pyrex bottles. Made of safe Pyrex resistant glass, they are unsurpassed in withstanding quick changes from hot to cold water.

Other features for which doctors approve F rex Nursing Bottles and mothers find them such a comfort and convenience are these:

6-sided—do not easily slip from your hand or from baby's. There are no sharp angles on the inside of the bottle. It is rounded off broadly so that it is very easy to clean.

Flat-bottomed—Pyrex Nursing Bottles stand firmly.

Ounces and half ounces are plainly marked.

Get enough Pyrex Nursing Bottles for a full day's feeding from your druggist.

Items – *Canisters*

Four piece set
8 oz., 16 oz., 24 oz., 48 oz. $15.00
with box $20.00

Items – *Casseroles & Cinderella Bowls*

"Each bowl has a handle and spout and many, many uses."

Art Deco casserole with underliner, 1½ qt., $100.00
"Bullseye," 1½ qt., $65.00

White Pyrex oval casserole, #192, 1½ qt.
(This color is called clambroth by collectors.) $100.00

Cinderella casserole "Opening Night at Lincoln Center, Sept. 23, 1962," 1½ qt., $30.00

Cinderella oval casserole, #943, 1½ qt., $18.00

Serving bowl set, with candle warmer, 2½ qt., in box, c. 1950, $22.00

Cinderella oval divided server, #963, 1½ qt., w/cover, $16.00

Cinderella divided dish #963, 1½ qt., $16.00

2 qt., 1959, $14.00

1 qt., $10.00

Individual casserole, 8 oz., $9.00

Items – *Casseroles & Cinderella Bowls*

1 qt., $8.00

1 qt., $8.00
1½ pt., $6.00

Items – *Children's Dishes*

Aluminum specialty Chilton toys, Manitowoc, Wisconsin, USA. There are French words on the bottoms, so these may have been made for Canadian market.

Coffee pot (1)	$12.00
Cups (4)	$6.00 each
Saucers (4)	$2.00 each
Plates (4)	$5.00 each
Casseroles (4)	$10.00 each
Set	$125.00

Items – *Children's Dishes*

Mug, 10 oz., $25.00
Bowl, 8 oz., $30.00

Child's divided plate, $35.00
Mug, 10 oz., $25.00

Items – *Children's Dishes, Christmas*

Mug, $35.00
Bowl, 8 oz., $30.00

Mug, $35.00
Bowl, 8 oz., $30.00

Mug, $35.00
Bowl, 8 oz., $30.00

Mug, $30.00

Carafes
4½" $15.00
12¾", w/candle warmer $20.00
with box $28.00
14", with top and candle warmer .$20.00
13", w/candle warmer $16.00
9¾" $15.00

Carafe $15.00
Carafe, w/candle warmer $25.00
Carafe $18.00
Carafe, w/candle warmer $20.00
Mug $8.00

Seven smart, new Gifts...

Complete your Christmas list with these beautiful, new PYREX Casseroles and Beverage Servers!

1 **New PYREX Cradled Decorator Casserole** in beautiful turquoise with delicate white lace pattern. Has handsome brass-plated cradle and double candle warmer. Cover can be used as extra serving dish, or as a tile to protect your table. 2½ qt., **$5.95.**

2 **New PYREX Cradled Space-Saver Casserole** in smart yellow with black needlepoint pattern. Has attractive brass-plated cradle. Cover may be used as extra serving dish, or as a tile to protect the finish of the table. Holds 2 full quarts. Only **$4.95.**

These smart new PYREX ware items make ideal Christmas gifts for the modern woman . . . because they're so wonderfully practical as well as beautiful.

● **See these,** and a host of other great gift ideas—including modern PYREX ware Bowl Sets, Dinnerware Sets, Oven-Freezer-Server Sets, smart Range-top ware, and many other handsome casseroles—at your nearest PYREX ware dealer's!

3 **New PYREX DeLuxe Carafe,** with electric warming tray of gold-hued anodized aluminum that keeps beverage at right temperature for serving. Carafe has 22-kt. gold decorations with capacity markings. Holds 12 cups. Only **$9.95.**

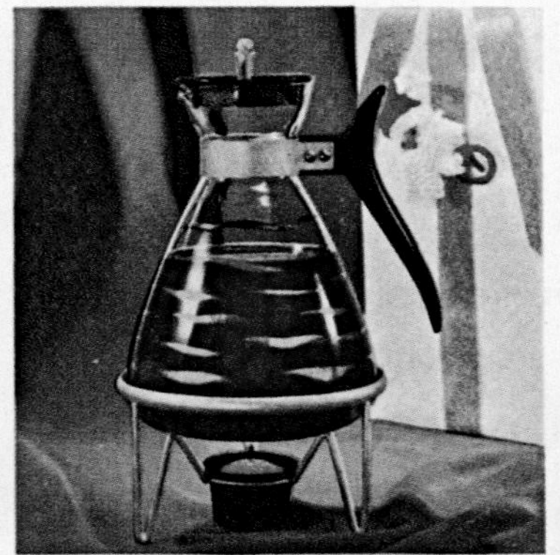

4 **New PYREX Carafe** with or without candle warmer and brass-plated base. Has 22-kt. gold decorations, capacity markings. 8-cup, **$2.95; with warmer, $3.95** —12 cup, **$3.95; with warmer, $4.95.**

5 **PYREX Instant Coffee and Tea Maker** has 22-kt. gold decorations, capacity markings. Many uses. 8-cup, with tea ball, **$3.95;** with warmer, **$5.95**— 12-cup, with tea ball, **$4.95;** with warmer, **$6.95.**

6 **New PYREX Cradled Decorator Casserole,** with beautiful black tulip pattern on white background, has smart, brass-plated cradle. Cover makes an extra serving dish, or may be used as a tile to protect the table finish. Holds 1½ quarts. Only **$3.95.**

7 **New PYREX Cradled Casserole** in smart egg shell white, with decorative brass-plated cradle. Cover is ideal for use as an extra storing or serving dish, or is equally handy when used as a tile to protect the table. Holds 1½ quarts. Only **$2.95.**

● **Each of these** beautiful PYREX ware items comes in an attractive box which you can easily gift wrap. The gay packages shown here are suggestions that may be helpful.

PYREX WARE

The perfect answer to your gift problems

THERE'S ONLY ONE **PYREX** BRAND WARE, A PRODUCT OF  CORNING GLASS WORKS, CORNING, NEW YORK

VISIT THE CORNING GLASS CENTER, CORNING, N. Y.

CORNING MEANS RESEARCH IN GLASS

Percolator	$35.00
Percolator	$40.00
Percolator	$30.00
Percolator	$25.00

Percolator, 6 cup, $35.00
With box, $40.00

Percolator, 9 cup, $35.00
With box, $45.00

Coffee Chemex,
with box, $30.00

TEA AND COFFEE TASTE BETTER WH

PLATINUM BANDED—GLASS LOCK-ON COVER—EBONY HANDLE

No.	Size	Pieces in Case	Weight Case Lbs.	Retail Price Each
84D-1	6 Cups	12	24	$1.95
84D-1	Bowl Only	12	16	1.20
84D-1	Cover Only			.45
84D-1	Handle Only			.25
84D-1	Metal Band			.25

GLASS LOCK-ON COVER—EBONY BLACK HANDLE

No.	Size	Pieces in Case	Weight Case Lbs.	Retail Price Each	Price Engraved Each
84	6 Cups	12	24	$1.49	$1.95
84	Bowl Only	12	16	.75	1.20
84	Cover Only			.35	
84	Handle Only			.25	
84	Metal Band			.25	

PLATINUM BANDED—CHROMIUM COVER AND HANDLE

No.	Size	Pieces in Case	Weight Case Lbs.	Retail Price Each
44D-1	6 Cups	12	19	$2.95
44D-1	Bowl Only	12	16	1.20
44D-1	Metal Cover and Band			1.75

CHROMIUM COVER AND HANDLE

No.	Size	Pieces in Case	Weight Case Lbs.	Retail Price Each	Price Engraved Each
44	6 Cups	12	19	$2.50	$2.95
44	Bowl Only	12	16	.75	1.20
44	Metal Cover and Band			1.75	

REPLACEMENT OFFER

Any glass part of a PYREX brand Teapot, Percolator or CORNING brand Coffee Maker which breaks from heat within one year from date of purchase, when used according to instructions, may be replaced by any dealer in PYREX brand Ware *in exchange* for the broken pieces.

6

N BREWED IN PYREX BRAND GLASS

INDIVIDUAL WITH GLASS LOCK-ON COVER AND EBONY BLACK HANDLE

No.	Size	Pieces in Case	Weight Case Lbs.	Retail Price Each	Price Engraved Each
81	1 Cup	12	13	$1.00	$1.35
81	Bowl Only	12	10	.50	.85
81	Cover Only			.35	
81	Handle Only			.20	
81	Metal Band			.20	

PYREX BRAND CRYSTAL PERCOLATOR

Without Coffee Basket Assembly, may be used as a Teapot; for boiling liquids, and as a milk pitcher or beverage server for hot or cold drinks.

No.	Description	Size	Pieces in Case	Weight Case Lbs.	Retail Price Each
76	Percolator	6 Cups	12	36	$1.79
768	Pitcher and Cover (Without Coffee Basket Assembly)	6 Cups (1½ Qt.)	12	30	1.29
766	Aluminum Coffee Basket Assembly				.50
76	Glass Bottom Only				.80
76	Glass Cover Only				.25
76	Glass Handle Only				.25
76	Metal Band Only				.25

PLATINUM BANDED CORNING BRAND COFFEE MAKER

No.	Size	Pieces in Case	Weight Case Lbs.	Retail Price Each
66D-1	6 Cups	6	25	$3.95
66D-1	Lower Glass Bowl Only			1.20
66D-1	Cover Only			.45

For prices on Upper Glass Bowl Only, Handle, Metal Band and Filter Plate see No. 66 Coffee Maker.

Packed in Distinctive Silver and Blue Gift Box

CORNING BRAND COFFEE MAKER

No.	Size	Pieces in Case	Weight Case Lbs.	Retail Price Each
66	6 Cups	6	25	$3.50
66	Upper Glass Bowl Only			1.40
66	Lower Glass Bowl Only			.75
66	Glass Cover Only			.35
66	Handle Only			.25
66	Metal Band Only			.25
66	Glass Filter Plate			.85

Packed in Distinctive Silver and Blue Gift Box

INSTRUCTIONS

CORNING BRAND ALL GLASS COFFEE MAKER

Use moderate heat, low to medium flame and low to medium electric power for reheating coffee in the lower bowl (server). Never allow bowl to boil dry. Should bowl boil dry do not add water until the glass is cool. Empty bowl should not be placed or left on hot burners. Set hot bowl on dry surfaces only. Use reasonable care in washing and handling the parts, to avoid mechanical breakage.

PYREX BRAND CRYSTAL PERCOLATOR

Use moderate heat, low to medium flame and low to medium electric power. Avoid boiling dry. Never allow the glass bowl to boil dry. Always add water to percolator *before* placing it over flame or electric element. Should percolator boil dry, do not add water until glass is cool. Empty percolator should not be placed or left on hot burners. Set hot percolator on dry surfaces only. Use reasonable care in washing and handling the parts, to avoid mechanical breakage.

7

Cruet set, $12.00
With box, $15.00

Insulators, $5.00 each

Juice carafe, $15.00
Juice carafe, $15.00

Juice carafes,
$15.00 each

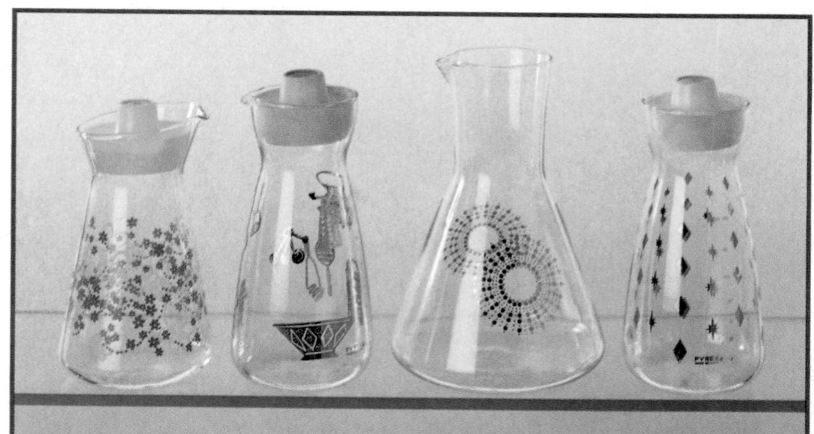

Bottle with stopper, 4½", $12.00

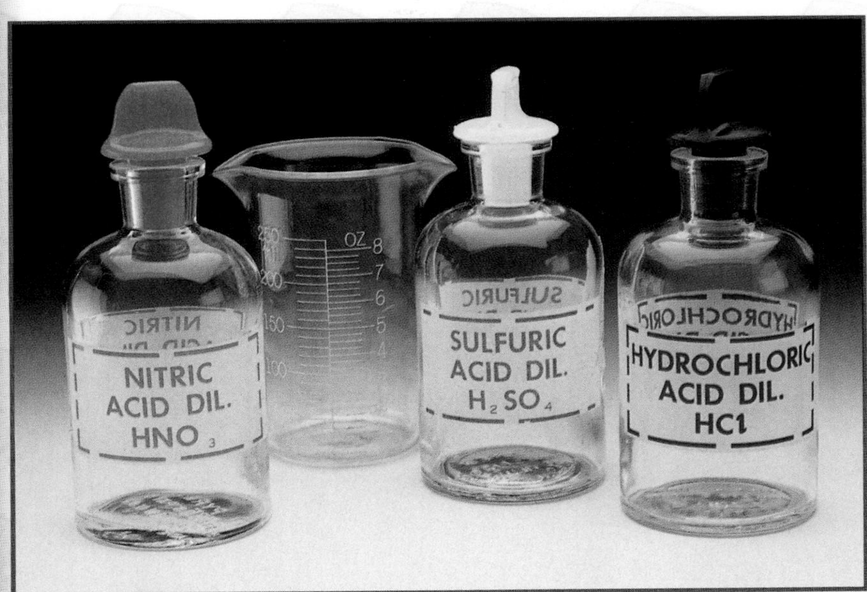

Beakers, with measurements

Item	Price
Nitric Acid	$10.00
Graduated	$12.00
Sulfuric Acid	$10.00
Hydrochloric Acid	$10.00

FREE NEW MEASURING CUP AND GRADUATE DISPLAY STAND

(Offer expires May 1, 1940)

This attractive colorful stand (Form D-86) size 14½" high x 16⅞" wide, is built to sell the new complete line of PYREX graduates and measures. Cutouts hold the Nos. 8 and 18 Measuring Cups. Nos. 597 and 598 graduates are attractively illustrated by photographs.

AND MEASURES . . . WITH FREE STAND ABOVE

GRADUATES

No. 597—BLOWN Permanent accurate red graduations

No. 598—PRESSED Accurate inside graduations

No.	U. S. Trade Size	Pieces in Case	Weight Case Lbs.	Retail Price Each
597	32 oz. (1 qt.)	12	12	$1.00
*598	16 oz.	12	15	.75

No. 597 packed in individual display box

*No. 598 cell packing

FUNNEL

No.	U. S. Trade Size	Pieces in Case	Weight Case Lbs.	Retail Price Each
*596	3"	12	4	$ .35

*Cell Packing

For easy filling of nursing bottles or transfer of any liquids. Easy to sterilize and keep clean.

9

Pyrex

Top row:		**Bottom row:**	
Dry measure (no spout), 1 cup	$20.00	8 cup	$12.00
4 cup	$12.00	1 cup	$10.00
2 cup	$10.00	1 cup	$10.00
2 cup	$10.00	8 cup	$12.00

Magic Chef dry measure, 1 cup, $35.00

Magic Chef dry measure, another view

Red, 2 cup, $100.00

Hamilton Beach, $12.00

Rainbow Stripe	
1½ pt., yellow	$18.00
2½ qt., yellow	$20.00
2½ qt., brown	$15.00

New Dot	
2½ qt., blue	$22.00
1½ pt., red	$20.00

Unidentified	
4 qt.	$12.00
2½ qt.	$10.00
1½ pt.	$8.00

"Garland"	
Cinderella bowl, 4 qt.	$14.00
Cinderella bowl, 2½ qt.	$12.00
Creamer	$6.00
Shakers, pair	$8.00

"Garland"	
Cinderella bowl, 1½ qt.	$10.00
Butter dish, 1¼ lb.	$12.00

Mixing bowl, #404,
4 qt., $12.00

Mug, front view, $20.00

Mug, back view

Pyrex beakers mug, $18.00

Eagle mug, 10 oz., $8.00

Mugs, 10 oz., $5.00 each
Flag or advertising mug, $15.00

Item	Price
Mug, 10 oz.	$4.00
Cup, 10 oz.	$3.00
Mug, 10 oz.	$6.00

10 oz., $6.00

Coffee cups, $6.00 each

IT'S EASIER TO BE A BETTER COOK

SAUCEPANS

No.	U. S. Trade Size	Outside Dimensions in Inches	Pieces in Case	Weight Case Lbs.	Retail Price Each Black Handle	Retail Price Each Chrome Handle
6832 (with handle)	1 qt.	6⅞x2¾	12	23	$ .95	$1.10
6833 (with handle)	1½ qt.	7⅞x3	12	28	1.25	1.40

SKILLET

No.	U. S. Trade Size	Outside Dimensions in Inches	Pieces in Case	Weight Case Lbs.	Retail Price Each Black Handle	Retail Price Each Chrome Handle
6817 (with handle)	1 pt.	7x1½	12	18	$ .75	$ .90

NO. 265 FLAMEWARE SET

2 Saucepans—1 qt. and 1½ qt. Capacity
7 inch Skillet—1 Removable Chrome Handle

No.	Pieces in Set	Sets Per Case	Approx. Wt. Case Lbs.	Retail Price Per Set
265	3	6	30	$2.65

GLASS ONLY AND HANDLES ONLY FOR PYREX FLAMEWARE

No.	Description	Retail Price Each
6817	Glass Only	$ .50
6832	Glass Only	.70
6833	Glass Only	1.00
	Black Handle	.30
	Chrome Handle	.45

• • •

Marks in the body of this glass are incidental to the process of manufacture and are not in any way detrimental to the use of the ware.

DOUBLE BOILERS

No.	U. S. Trade Size	Outside Dimensions in Inches	Pieces in Case	Weight Case Lbs.	Retail Price Each
6762	1 qt.	6 1/16 wide x 7½ high	6	29	$3.45
6763	1½ qt.	6½ wide x 8¼ high	6	34	3.95
6762	Cover Only				.40
6763	Cover Only				.50
6762	Upper Bowl Only				.85
6763	Upper Bowl Only				1.05
6762	Lower Bowl Only				1.00
6763	Lower Bowl Only				1.20
6762, 6763	Glass Handle Only—(Single)				.45
6762, 6763	Metal Band and Sleeve for Each Handle				.35

REPLACEMENT OFFER

Any glass part of a PYREX brand Flameware dish which breaks from heat within one year from date of purchase, when used according to instructions, may be replaced by any dealer in PYREX brand Ware *in exchange* for the broken pieces.

8

Pyrex

Top row:
With handle . . . .$25.00 each
Bottom row:
Saucepan, 1 qt. $20.00
Skillet, 1 pt., 7" $18.00
Saucepan, 1½ qt. $22.00

Dinnerware Patterns – *"Blue & Yellow Flowers"*

Item	Price
Creamer	$5.00
Sugar	$8.00
Cup	$3.00

Dinnerware Patterns – *"Blue Onion"*

Item	Price
Mug, 10 oz.	$4.00
Cup	$3.00
Gravy	$12.00

Dinnerware Patterns – *Flamingo*

Item	Price
Plate, 8¼", salad	$3.00
Plate, 10", dinner	$5.00
Saucer	$1.00
Bowl, 6¼", cereal	$5.00

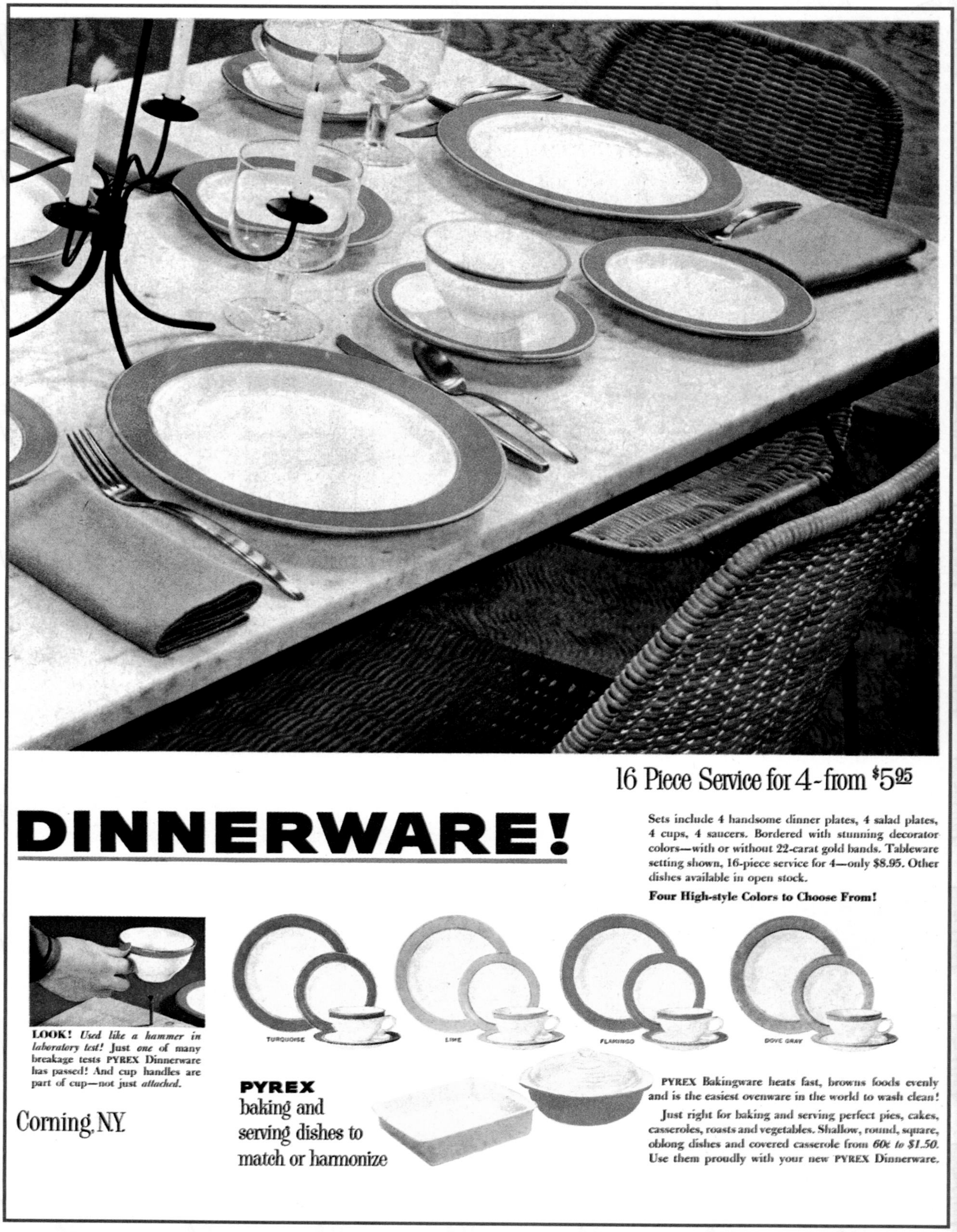

16 Piece Service for 4 - from $5.95

DINNERWARE!

Sets include 4 handsome dinner plates, 4 salad plates, 4 cups, 4 saucers. Bordered with stunning decorator colors—with or without 22-carat gold bands. Tableware setting shown, 16-piece service for 4—only $8.95. Other dishes available in open stock.

Four High-style Colors to Choose From!

LOOK! *Used like a hammer in laboratory test!* Just *one* of many breakage tests PYREX Dinnerware has passed! And cup handles are part of cup—not just *attached*.

Corning, N.Y.

PYREX
baking and serving dishes to match or harmonize

PYREX Bakingware heats fast, browns foods evenly and is the easiest ovenware in the world to wash clean!

Just right for baking and serving perfect pies, cakes, casseroles, roasts and vegetables. Shallow, round, square, oblong dishes and covered casserole from *60¢ to $1.50.* Use them proudly with your new PYREX Dinnerware.

Dinnerware Patterns – *"Laurel Band"*

Plate, salad	$2.00
Plate, dinner	$4.00
Bowl, 6¼", cereal	$3.00
Saucer	$.50
Cup	$1.50

Dinnerware Patterns – *Lime*

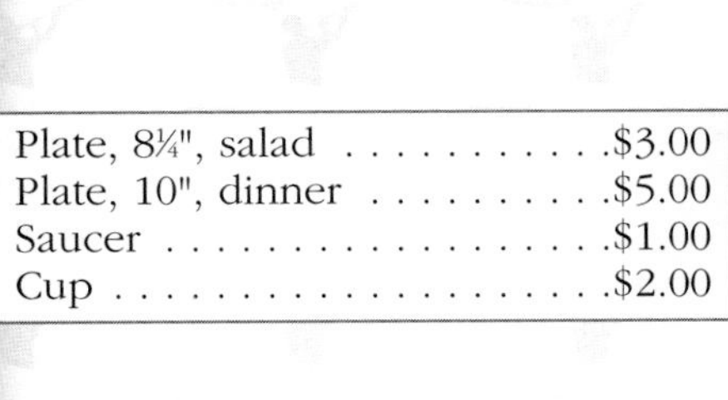

Plate, 8¼", salad	$3.00
Plate, 10", dinner	$5.00
Saucer	$1.00
Cup	$2.00

Dinnerware Patterns – *"Vegetables"*

Sugar (sugar lid plastic), $6.00
Creamer, $4.00

Dinnerware Patterns – *"Wheat"*

Gravy, with liner, $15.00

Dinnerware Patterns – *"Western"*

Plate, 6$\frac{13}{16}$", $4.00

Mug, $8.00

Dinnerware Patterns – *Unidentified*

Dinner plate, $4.00
Cereal bowl, $2.50

Commemorative plate, $8.00

Plate, salad, Bradford House	$4.00
Plate, dinner	$5.00
Cup	$2.00

Plate, 9", dinner	$3.00
Platter, 12½"	$7.00
Bowl, 5", cereal	$2.50

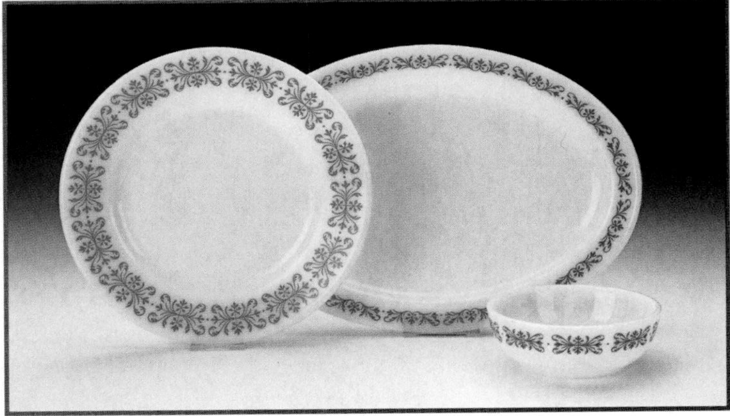

Platter, 11", $7.00

Pyr-O-Rex (imitation of Pyrex) lid

Older Dinnerware – *Chinex Classic*

MacBeth-Evans Division of Corning Glass Works, Late 1930s – early 1940s

Colors: Ivory, ivory with decal decoration

Plain Ivory			
7 Bowl, 5¾", cereal	$5.50	5 Creamer	$5.00
Bowl, 6¾", salad	$12.00	2 Cup	$4.50
Bowl, 7", vegetable	$14.00	9 Plate, 6¼", sherbet	$2.50
Bowl, 7¾", soup	$12.50	6 Plate, 9¾", dinner	$4.00
Bowl, 9", vegetable	$11.00	4 Plate, 11½", sandwich or cake	$7.50
Bowl, 11"	$17.00	3 Saucer	$2.00
Butter dish	$55.00	8 Sherbet, low footed	$7.00
Butter dish bottom	$12.50	1 Sugar	$5.00
Butter dish top	$42.50		

Bouquet

Princess

Bouquet and Princess

Key	Item	Price
10	Bowl, 5¾", cereal	$10.00
	Bowl, 6¾", salad	$20.00
	Bowl, 7", vegetable	$25.00
	Bowl, 7¾", soup	$25.00
6	Bowl, 9", vegetable	$25.00
	Bowl, 11"	$35.00
	Butter dish	$75.00
	Butter dish bottom	$27.50
2	Butter dish top	$47.50
3	Creamer	$10.00
8	Cup	$6.50
7	Plate, 6¼", sherbet	$4.00
4	Plate, 9¾", dinner	$9.00
5	Plate, 11½", sandwich or cake	$15.00
9	Saucer	$4.00
	Sherbet, low footed	$11.00
1	Sugar	$10.00

Rose Blue

Key	Item	Price
4	Bowl, 5¾", cereal	$10.00
	Bowl, 6¾", salad	$20.00
	Bowl, 7", vegetable	$25.00
	Bowl, 7¾", soup	$25.00
5	Bowl, 9", vegetable	$25.00
	Bowl, 11"	$35.00
	Butter dish	$75.00
	Butter dish bottom	$27.50
	Butter dish top	$47.50
	Creamer	$10.00
1	Cup	$6.50
2	Plate, 6¼", sherbet	$4.00
6	Plate, 9¾", dinner	$9.00
3	Plate, 11½", sandwich or cake	$15.00
	Saucer	$4.00
	Sherbet, low footed	$11.00
7	Sugar	$10.00

	Rose Pink				
10	Bowl, 5¾", cereal	$10.00	2	Cup	$6.50
	Bowl, 6¾", salad	$20.00	6	Cup, demitasse	$8.00
	Bowl, 7", vegetable	$25.00	8	Egg cup	$7.50
	Bowl, 7¾", soup	$25.00	1	Plate, 6¼", sherbet	$4.00
	Bowl, 9", vegetable	$25.00	9	Plate, 9¾", dinner	$9.00
	Bowl, 11"	$35.00	5	Plate, 11½", sandwich or cake	$15.00
	Butter dish	$75.00	3	Saucer	$4.00
	Butter dish bottom	$27.50	7	Saucer, demitasse	$2.00
	Butter dish top	$47.50		Sherbet, low footed	$11.00
4	Creamer	$10.00		Sugar	$10.00

Older Dinnerware – *Chinex Classic*

Windsor Blue

No.	Item	Price
5	Bowl, 5¾", cereal	$18.00
1	Bowl, 6¾", salad	$40.00
	Bowl, 7", vegetable	$40.00
	Bowl, 7¾", soup	$40.00
	Bowl, 9", vegetable	$40.00
	Bowl, 11"	$45.00
	Butter dish	$150.00
2	Butter dish bottom	$50.00
	Butter dish top	$100.00
	Creamer	$20.00
8	Cup	$15.00
6	Plate, 6¼", sherbet	$7.50
7	Plate, 9¾", dinner	$20.00
3	Plate, 11½", sandwich or cake	$30.00
9	Saucer	$6.00
4	Sherbet, low footed	$27.50
	Sugar	$20.00

Windsor Brown	
2 Bowl, 5¾", cereal .$18.00	Creamer .$20.00
Bowl, 6¾", salad .$40.00	Cup .$15.00
Bowl, 7", vegetable .$40.00	1 Plate, 6¼", sherbet .$7.50
Bowl, 7¾", soup .$40.00	3 Plate, 9¾", dinner .$20.00
Bowl, 9", vegetable .$40.00	Plate, 11½", sandwich or cake .$30.00
Bowl, 11" .$45.00	Saucer .$6.00
Butter dish .$150.00	4 Sherbet, low footed .$27.50
Butter dish bottom .$50.00	Sugar .$20.00
Butter dish top .$100.00	

Older Dinnerware – *Cremax*

MacBeth-Evans Division of Corning Glass Works, Late 1930s – early 1940s

Colors: Cremax, Cremax with fired-on colored trim or decals

Bordette and Windsor

Key	Item	Price
	Bowl, 5¾", cereal	$12.00
	Bowl, 7¾", soup	$25.00
	Bowl, 9", vegetable	$22.00
	Creamer	$10.00
6	Cup	$5.00
1	Cup, demitasse	$25.00
	Egg cup, 2¼"	$12.00
5	Plate, 6¼", bread and butter	$4.00
3	Plate, 9¾", dinner	$14.00
4	Plate, 11½", sandwich	$22.00
7	Saucer	$3.50
2	Saucer, demitasse	$10.00
	Sugar, open	$10.00

Add 50% for castle decal.

Plain (also available; not shown)

Item	Price
Bowl, 5¾", cereal	$4.00
Bowl, 7¾", soup	$7.50
Bowl, 9", vegetable	$12.00
Creamer	$4.50
Cup	$4.00
Cup, demitasse	$11.00
Egg cup, 2¼"	$12.00
Plate, 6¼", bread and butter	$2.00
Plate, 9¾", dinner	$4.50
Plate, 11½", sandwich	$5.50
Saucer	$1.00
Saucer, demitasse	$4.00
Sugar, open	$4.50

Princess and Rose

Item	Price
Bowl, 5¾", cereal	$12.00
Bowl, 7¾", soup	$25.00
Bowl, 9", vegetable	$22.00
Creamer	$10.00
6 Cup	$5.00
Cup, demitasse	$25.00
8 Egg cup, 2¼"	$12.00
Plate, 6¼", bread and butter	$4.00
3 Plate, 9¾", dinner	$14.00
4 Plate, 11½", sandwich	$22.00
7 Saucer	$3.50
Saucer, demitasse	$10.00
Sugar, open	$10.00

Add 50% for castle decal.

Sugar, unidentified pattern, $12.00

Blue (2 shades)			
8 Bowl, 7¾", soup	$20.00	4 Plate, 6¼", bread and butter	$7.00
6 Creamer	$15.00	Plate, 8", salad	$10.00
2 Cup	$10.00	9 Plate, 9¾", dinner	$15.00
5 Mug	$20.00	3 Saucer	$4.00
7 Pitcher, milk	$40.00	1 Sugar, open	$15.00

9⅞" . . . .$6.00 each
8⅜" . . . .$5.00 each
7" . . . .$4.00 each

10", blue $6.00
8⅜", red $5.00
7⅛", yellow $4.00

Cobalt blue
10" $9.00
8½" $7.00
7½" $4.00

8", $3.00

Top row:		**Bottom row:**	
Casserole, 2 qt.	$6.00	Pie plate	$3.00
Platter, 13"	$6.00	Utility dish, 11"	$4.00
		Baker, 9", oval	$4.00

9⅞",	$6.00
8⅜",	$5.00
7"	$4.00

Bowl, 7⁷⁄₁₆"	$2.00
Plate, 7⁷⁄₁₆"	$1.00
Plate, 10⅝"	$3.00

Rectangular baker, 11", $6.00
Round baker, 8⅞", $7.00
Casserole lid, 8⅝", $3.00

Recent Microwaveables

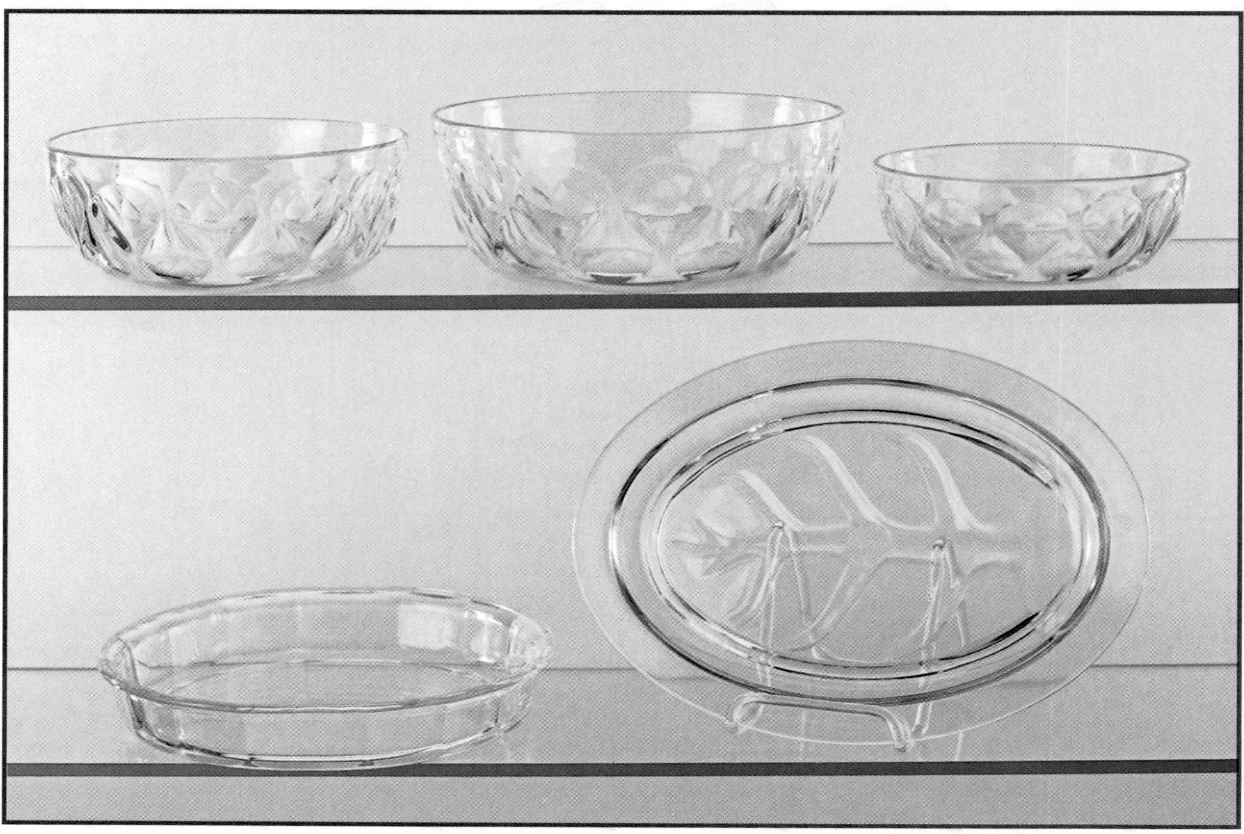

Crystal			
Top row:		**Bottom row:**	
"Diamond" Bowls		Pie plate, 9"	$6.00
8⅜"	$3.00	Plate, 13", Tree of Life	$12.00
9⅞"	$5.00		
7"	$2.00		

Top row:
- Butter dish, ¼ lb. $4.00
- Casserole, 10 oz., individual $5.00
- Bowl, 1½ pt. $3.00
- Custard, 4 oz. $3.00
- Custard, 4 oz. $3.00
- Bowl, 4 qt. $6.00

Bottom row:
- Baker, with box $5.00
- Bowls . . . .$2.00 each
  - With lids . . . .$3.00 each
- Divided dish $4.00

Recent Microwaveables

Pyrex Portables, with hot pack, 4-piece, 12.00

Pyrex Portables, bowl, with lid, $10.00

Pyrex Portables, personal size, 4-piece, $12.00

Napkin rings, $3.00 each
Six in box, $25.00

Pyrex lid, made in France, $10.00

English Pyrex, mark of Crown	
Bowl, 10⅝"	$8.00
Bowl, 9⅜"	$6.00
Skillet	$15.00
Bowl, 5¼"	$12.00
Gravy	$10.00

Casserole, 8¾", $15.00

English set in box, $22.00

Foreign Patterns – *"Blue Willow,"* England

Key	Item	Price
	Bowl, 4½", dessert	$12.00
	Bowl, 6", cereal	$15.00
6	Bowl, 10", soup	$20.00
	Casserole, 1 pt., with cover	$18.00
	Casserole, 1 qt., with cover	$22.50
7	Casserole, 2 qt., with cover	$30.00
1	Gravy boat	$25.00
2	Gravy boat platter	$12.50
5	Plate, 8"	$12.00
3	Plate, 10"	$20.00
4	Plate, 12"	$25.00
	Platter, 13"	$42.50

Foreign Patterns – *Tally Ho,* *mfg. James A. Jobling & Co. Limited, England*

Bowl, 4½", dessert $10.00
2 Bowl, 6", cereal $12.50
3 Bowl, 5", mixing $10.00
8 Bowl, 7", mixing $12.50
7 Bowl, 8", mixing $15.00
Bowl, 8", vegetable $20.00
Bowl, 9", mixing $18.00
14 Bowl, 9", soup $15.00
1 Casserole, 1 pt., with cover $18.00
15 Casserole, 1½ qt., with cover $22.50
Casserole, 2 qt., with cover $30.00
9 Creamer $12.50
5 Cup $8.00
10 Gravy boat $20.00
Gravy boat platter $10.00
16 Plate, 8" $9.00
11 Plate, 10" $15.00
12 Plate, 12" $20.00
4 Platter, 13" $25.00
6 Saucer $3.00
Sugar $12.50

Retail Prices Effective August 15, 1938
PYREX
BRAND
OVENWARE • FLAMEWARE
CORNING GLASS WORKS... CORNING, N.Y.

PYREX Color Ware Oven-and-Table Set

2½-quart bowl for main dish; four 12-ounce dishes for soup, or dessert. Useful! Beautiful! Red or yellow.

Complete set **$2.95**

PYREX Casserole with Utility Cover

Bakes perfectly—keeps food hot! Cover doubles as extra dish. 1½-quart size, 89¢; 2-quart size, $1.00.

1-quart size **79¢**

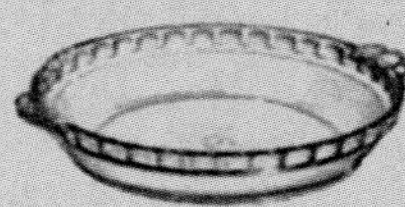

PYREX Flavor-Saver Pie Plates

High rim holds juice in. Oven stays clean. Bottom crust browns nicely. Note the handy handles! 10-inch size, 69¢.

9-inch size **59¢**

PYREX Color Ware Oven and Refrigerator Set

They stack to save space in storing. Clear covers to see through. Use dishes for baking, and serving, too.

Complete set **$2.95**

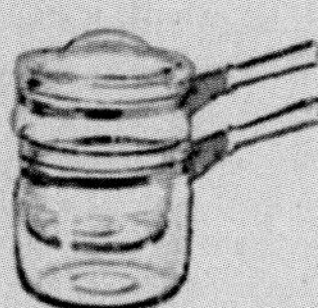

PYREX Double Boiler

No boiling dry—you can see the water level! Ideal for frostings, sauces. Use top and bottom separately as saucepans.

1½-quart size **$3.45**

Be sure it's

PYREX

BRAND WARE ®

Look for "PYREX" in the glass

PYREX Measures

For hot or cold liquids. For making baby's formula. Easy for measuring and pouring—easy to clean. 1-cup size, 29¢; 1-quart size, 79¢.

1-pint size **59¢**

PYREX Round Cake Dish

Buy *two* for high, light layer cakes! Right size for prepared mixes. Browns so well! Perfect for biscuits, scalloped vegetables, too.

8-inch size **59¢**

PYREX Color Ware Hostess Set

For baking and serving! Food cooks so well—looks so good! 1½-quart covered casserole and four 7-ounce ramekins. Red or yellow, gift-boxed.

Complete set **$2.95**

PYREX Custard Cups

Individual Pyrex Ware dishes come in four sizes . . . you'll want some of each! 6½-ounce size, 10¢; 9½-ounce size, 15¢; 15-ounce size, 19¢.

5-ounce size **10¢**

PYREX Utility Dish

For baking cakes, biscuits, baked apples, macaroni 'n cheese! Keeps food hot—a dream to clean. 2-quart size, 89¢; 3-quart size, $1.00.

1-quart size **69¢**

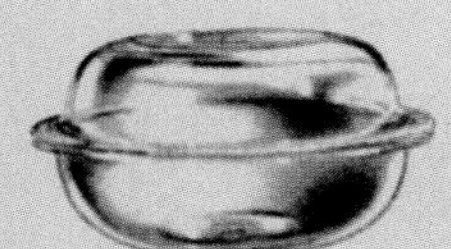

PYREX Oven Roaster

Big enough to roast a 5-lb. chicken! Watch a bird or roast while it cooks to perfection! Use as two separate baking dishes, too.

3-quart size **$1.39**

PYREX Mixing Bowls

Rounded inside for easiest mixing by hand or electric mixer. Flat bases for steadiness. Three handy sizes for mixing, baking, and serving.

Nest of 3 **$1.39**

PYREX Pie Plates

The best-loved pie plates of all. They bake so well; look so nice; wash clean! 6-inch size, 19¢; 9-inch size, 39¢; 10-inch size, 49¢.

8-inch size **29¢**

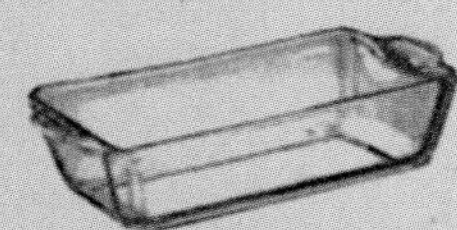

PYREX Loaf Pan

Just what you need for meat loaf, nut bread, baked beans! The handles are a blessing! Foods never taste of the pan! 10½-inch size, 89¢.

9-inch size **69¢**

PYREX WARE—A PRODUCT OF CORNING GLASS WORKS

Visit the Glass Center—Library, Museum, Glass-making—Corning, N. Y. Open daily Except Monday.

with PYREX Ware

"PYREX" is a registered trade-mark in the U. S. of Corning Glass Works, Corning, N. Y.

Are you missing any of these PYREX dishes?

A joy to cook with! Easy to wash clean! So smart for serving!

PYREX FLAMEWARE PERCOLATOR

Don't guess—*see* your coffee perk to just the right strength! Cover locks on for safe pouring. 4-cup size, $2.45; 6-cup size, $2.95. 9-cup size, **$3.45**

PYREX SHALLOW BAKING AND SERVING DISH

Serve your pies in new PYREX Bakingware that's as smart as your table china. Lime green or flamingo red, milk-white inside. 8½-inch size, **60¢**

PYREX LOAF PAN

Quick, even baking for hot breads, meat or fish loaf. PYREX Ware is as easy to wash clean as a dinner plate. 8¾-inch size, 69¢. 10¼-inch size, **89¢**

PYREX FLAMEWARE DOUBLE BOILER

You can see the water level at a glance. Use as two separate saucepans —cover fits both. Hang-up rings save storage space. 1½-quart size, **$3.45**

PYREX ROUND BAKING AND SERVING DISH

Colorful PYREX Bakingware is *tempered* —this useful dish can go straight from refrigerator to oven to table. Lime or flamingo. 8¼-inch size, **95¢**

PYREX COLOR BOWL SET

Rounded inside for easy mixing by hand or electric mixer. Brightly colored bowls in four sizes: 1½-pint; 1½-, 2½- and 4-quart. Set of 4, **$2.95**

PYREX UTILITY DISH

For baking fish, apples, biscuits, cakes. Bakes perfectly, and it's so easy to wash clean! 3 sizes—2-quart, 89¢; 3-quart, $1.00. 1½-quart size, **69¢**

PYREX CASSEROLE WITH UTILITY COVER

The cover's an extra dish! PYREX Ware heats quickly, browns evenly, keeps foods hot! 3 sizes—1½-quart, 89¢; 2-quart, $1.00. 1-quart size, **79¢**

PYREX INDIVIDUAL DISHES

Handy clear individual dishes—every woman's favorite for baking, serving, storing. 5-ounce size, 5¢; 10-ounce, 15¢; 1-pint, 19¢. 6-ounce size, **10¢**

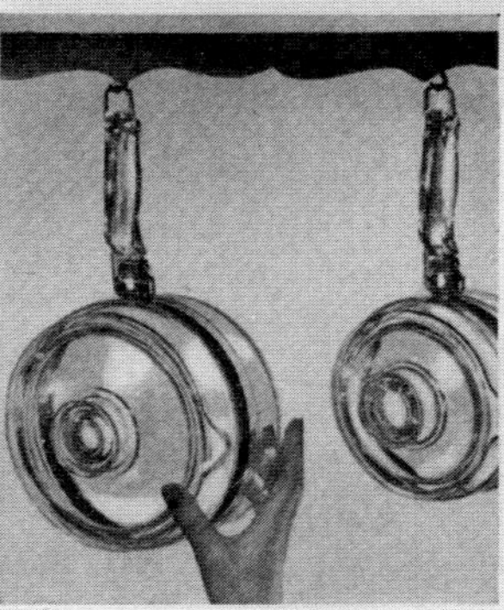

PYREX FLAMEWARE SAUCEPAN

PYREX Flameware saucepans have lock-on covers; stay-cool handles; hang-up rings for storing! 1½-quart, $2.25; 2-quart, $2.45. 1-quart size, **$1.95**

PYREX FLAMEWARE TEAPOT

Boil water, brew tea, serve proudly in the sturdy PYREX teapot. All PYREX Flameware is *tempered* to make it extra-strong and durable. 6-cup size, **$1.95**

PYREX OVEN AND REFRIGERATOR SET

Four gaily colored dishes with clear covers—dandy for baking, serving, storing. You'll find dozens of uses for these dishes. Set of four, **$2.95**

There's only one PYREX ware, a product of Corning Glass Works, Corning, N.Y.

VISIT THE CORNING GLASS CENTER, CORNING, N. Y.

Pyrex" is a registered trade-mark in the U. S. of Corning Glass Works, Corning, N. Y.

14

BETTER HOMES & GARDENS, FEBRUARY, 1953

ABOUT THE AUTHORS

Gene M. Florence, Jr., a native Kentuckian, graduated from the University of Kentucky in 1967. He held a double major in mathematics and English that he immediately put to use, first in industry and subsequently, in teaching junior and senior high school.

A collector since childhood, Mr. Florence progressed from baseball cards, comic books, coins, and bottles to glassware. His buying and selling glassware "hobby" began to override his nine-year teaching career. In the summer of 1972, he wrote a book on Depression glassware that was well received by collectors in the field, persuading him in 1976 to leave teaching and pursue the antique glass business full time. This allowed time to travel to glass shows throughout the country, where he assiduously studied the prices of glass being sold — and those of that glass remaining unsold.

Cathy Gaines Florence, also a native Kentuckian, graduated with honors and a coveted voice award from high school, attended Georgetown College, where she obtained a French major and an English minor, and then married her middle-school sweetheart, Gene Florence.

She taught four years at the middle-school level, then worked part-time while raising two boys. It was then that she typed her husband's first manuscript, written in "chicken scratch." The first three or four letters of each word would be legible, and then it was up to her to guess what the last were. To both Gene and Cathy's astonishment, the book sold well, and a new career was born for her husband. Their lives took different turns from the teaching careers they'd planned.

In the mid-80s, Cathy authored a book on collecting quilts, harking back to skills taught her by her grandmothers; she has since coauthored books on glass with husband Gene.

Books written by the Florences include the following titles: *The Collector's Encyclopedia of Depression Glass*, *Stemware Identification*, *The Collector's Encyclopedia of Akro Agate*, *Pocket Guide to Depression Glass & More*, *Kitchen Glassware of the Depression Years*; *Collectible Glassware from the 40s, 50s, and 60s*; *Glass Candlesticks of the Depression Era*, *Anchor Hocking's Fire-King & More*, *Florences' Glassware Pattern Identification Guide* I – IV, *Florence's Big Book of Salt and Pepper Shakers*, *Standard Baseball Card Price Guide*, six editions of *Very Rare Glassware of the Depression Years*, and *Treasures of Very Rare Depression Glass*. Gene has also written six volumes of *The Collector's Encyclopedia of Occupied Japan* and a book on Degenhart glassware for that museum. The Florences' most recent books are *Florences' Glass Kitchen Shakers, 1930 – 1950s* and *The Hazel-Atlas Glass Identification and Value Guide*.

More Titles by *Gene & Cathy Florence*

NEWEST EDITION

COLLECTOR'S ENCYCLOPEDIA OF DEPRESSION GLASS, SEVENTEENTH EDITION

Item #6830 • ISBN: 1-57432-469-1 • 8½ x 11 • 256 Pgs. • HB • $19.95

COLLECTIBLE GLASSWARE FROM THE 40S, 50S & 60S, EIGHTH EDITION

Item #6821 • ISBN: 1-57432-460-8 • 8½ x 11 • 256 Pgs. • HB • $19.95

TREASURES OF VERY RARE DEPRESSION GLASS

Item #6241• ISBN: 1-57432-336-9 • 8½ x 11 • 368 Pgs. • HB • $39.95

ELEGANT GLASSWARE OF THE DEPRESSION ERA, ELEVENTH EDITION

Item #6559 • ISBN: 1-57432-417-9 • 8½ x 11 • 256 Pgs. • HB • $24.95

KITCHEN GLASSWARE OF THE DEPRESSION YEARS, SIXTH EDITION

Item #5827 • ISBN: 1-57432-220-6 • 8½ x 11 • 272 Pgs. • HB • $24.95

POCKET GUIDE TO DEPRESSION GLASS & MORE, FOURTEENTH EDITION

Item #6556 • ISBN: 1-57432-414-4 • 5½ x 8½ • 224 Pgs • PB • $12.95

FLORENCES' GLASSWARE
PATTERN IDENTIFICATION GUIDES

Vol. I • Item #5042 • ISBN: 1-57432-045-9
8½ x 11 • 176 Pgs. • PB • $18.95

Vol. II • Item #5615 • ISBN: 1-57432-177-3
8½ x 11 • 208 Pgs. • PB • $19.95

Vol. III • Item #6142 • ISBN: 1-57432-315-6
8½ x 11 • 272 Pgs. • PB • $19.95

Vol. IV • Item #6643 • ISBN: 1-57432-451-9
8½ x 11 • 208 Pgs. • PB • $19.95

THE HAZEL-ATLAS GLASS
IDENTIFICATION AND VALUE GUIDE

Item #6562 • ISBN: 1-57432-420-9 • 8½ x 11 • 224 Pgs. • HB • $24.95

GLASS CANDLESTICKS OF THE DEPRESSION ERA

Item #5354 • ISBN: 1-57432-136-6 • 8½ x 11 • 176 Pgs. • HB • $24.95

ANCHOR HOCKING'S FIRE-KING & MORE,
SECOND EDITION

Item #5602 • ISBN: 1-57432-164-1 • 8½ x 11 • 224 Pgs. • HB • $24.95

FLORENCES' GLASS KITCHEN SHAKERS, 1930 – 1950S

Item #6462 • ISBN: 1-57432-389-X • 8½ x 11 • 160 Pgs • PB • $19.95

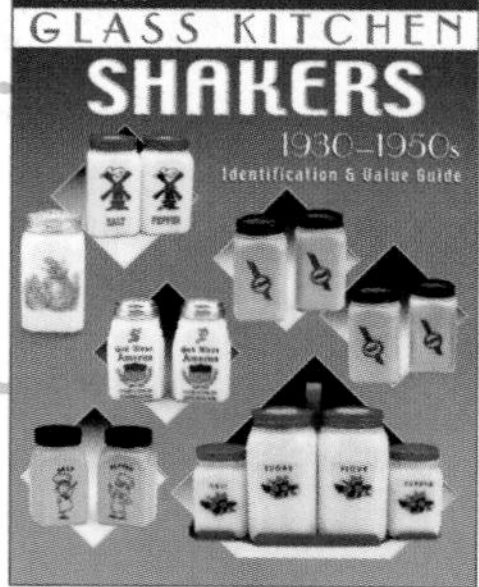

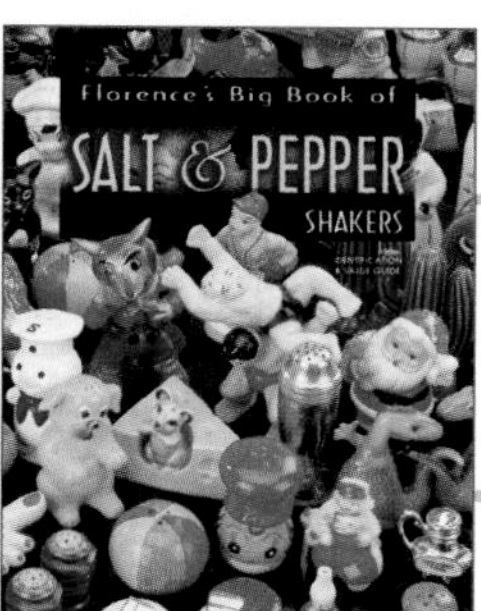

FLORENCES' BIG BOOK OF SALT & PEPPER SHAKERS

Item #5918 • ISBN: 1-57432-257-5 • 8½ x 11 • 272 Pgs. • PB • $24.95

Schroeder's ANTIQUES Price Guide

...is the #1 bestselling antiques & collectibles value guide on the market today, and here's why...

- More than 400 advisors, well-known dealers, and top-notch collectors work together with our editors to bring you accurate information regarding pricing and identification.
- More than 50,000 items in over 500 categories are listed along with hundreds of sharp original photos that illustrate not only the rare and unusual, but the common, popular collectibles as well.
- Each large close-up shot shows important details clearly. Every subject is represented with histories and background information, a feature not found in any of our competitors' publications.
- Our editors keep abreast of newly developing trends, often adding several new categories a year as the need arises.

Without doubt, you'll find
Schroeder's Antiques Price Guide
the only one to buy for reliable information and values.

If it merits the interest of today's collector, you'll find it in Schroeder's. And you can feel confident that the information we publish is up-to-date and accurate. Our advisors thoroughly check each category to spot inconsistencies, listings that may not be entirely reflective of market dealings, and lines too vague to be of merit. Only the best of the lot remains for publication.

COLLECTOR BOOKS
P.O. Box 3009
Paducah, KY 42002–3009
1-800-626-5420
www.collectorbooks.com